BROADMOOR SINISTER

SANCTUARY OR HELL FOR THE CRIMINALLY INSANE

BORIS COSTER

Prologue by

CHRISTOPHER BERRY-DEE

CONTENTS.

***

Prologue – by Christopher Berry-Dee

'There is a singular '*constant*': as strong as a steel wire it
threads continuously throughout every page of this book and
this '*constant*' is all about '**care**' - the provision of what is
necessary for the health, welfare, maintenance, and protection of
someone or something.
And, there has been a *constant* running throughout the care for
the mentally ill since Victorian time and this *constant* remains
in place to this very day.
Let that be said from the very outset of this book.'

Christopher Berry-Dee.

What an absolute delight! What a thrill it is for me to help realise the dream of dedicated researcher; a jolly nice chap is Boris who always wanted to write a book and he has cracked it in one – job done and dusted!

I met Boris on Facebook: a great platform for meeting people from all walks of life, colour, creed, religion and, if you have your wits about you, it's a great place to meet future business partners, develop your ideas with them and network like crazy.

So it was in FB that *our* Boris, with his great sense of Cockney dry, oft-times black humour, was posting online about the Broadmoor High-Security Hospital, Crowthorne, Berkshire, which has housed, still does, many of the most violently criminally insane, and this was right up my street, so please allow me to briefly explain.

For decades now I have been interviewing sadosexual homicidal psychopaths in prisons around the world so I know a thing or two about the mindsets of these sick humanoid beasts who prey on a men, women, children and in some cases have raped and murdered toddlers. I am the author of some 35 different titles, many are translated into other languages including Russian, Polish, German and Japanese. For the past three years I have been the UK's No. 1 best-selling true crime writer, a *Sunday Times* bestseller, and with tongue-in-cheek I am probably the best-selling true crime writer of all time worldwide With that established, I testify that I know a great idea for a book when I see one - *Broadmoor Sinister* ticks all of my boxes and pushes all of my buttons.

'Critics are like eunuchs in a harem: they know how it's done,
they've seen it done every day, but they are unable to do it themselves and
as utterly useless at a gang-bang'.

Brendan Francis Aiden Behan (1923-1964).

There are countless millions of aspiring writers across the world; and it is said that there is a good book in every one of us. Matching that figure are countless millions of critics who seem to know how it's done but cannot do it for themselves as the famous Irish poet once wrote. But us pensmiths write what *we* like, not what others *expect us* to write or what they like. We write to educate and please ourselves not others. So, with that in mind, and while Boris will undoubtedly draw heat, it will come only from those who have not got the balls to write a book themselves. I recall the words of John Osborne: 'Asking a working writer what he feels about critics is like asking a lamp-post what it feels about dogs'. Hear, hear, Sir, I jolly well say!

To finalize this Prologue, I need to say that when I started writing decades ago, my mentor was the great true crime historian and true crime writer Robin Odell, who in turn had written with the legendary Jo Gaute. So there is a literary DNA running throughout my career and I, of course, have been inspired, believe it not by the superb often hilariously funny travel writer Bill Bryson. Bill gives his readers mega fascinating facts and often he wanders off track into Trivia Land; all of which adds zing, sparkle. More importantly he doesn't talk at the reader he brings you along with him on his journeys as if you are so special you are his close friend too. This is a literary style I have developed over the years. It's great fun, it truly is.

Boris came 'Top-of-Class' in my YouTube *True Crime Writing Master Classes*, produced by the incredible, blue-chip TV documentary-making team at Rock Oyster Media. Charlotte and me go back several decades, for it was Charlotte who produced the famous 'Born to Kill' series for Twofour TV, in which I appeared as a consultant on serial homicide. Boris appears in 'Class No.6'. Indeed, he is already in huge Podcast demand, enjoying the unique experience of getting involved with the making of international TV, so if he can do it so can you.

Broadmoor Sinister is all about care. Boris writes from the heart; a very bold move for a first-time writer dipping his fingers into ink. He writes with Cockney pathos. He is a guy who came from the same street as the Krays. He has written this book because he truly 'cares', and Boris - like the boxer Kray twins - is not, as one might expect shy to pull his literary punches either.

Therefore, I am honoured having been given the opportunity to write this Prologue and if I were to look into a crystal ball, I predict many more books coming from him in the future. Congrats, Boris, well done you, sir.

Christopher Berry-Dee, investigative criminologist. Author and TV true crime consultant.

***

Introduction.

'Men will always be mad, and those who think they can cure them are the maddest of all.'

Voltaire: letter, 1962.

Why is one of the most publicaly-funded mental institutions in world history so shrouded in secrecy? What sick secrets hide behind the grim walls, and who are these highly-paid pen-pushing tax-paid folk trying to protect? Their negligence…utter incompetence…or, in some cases their own reputations, all the way up to High Government.

At the time of writing, Prime Minister Boris Johnson is mired neck deep in scandals; as bent as a Micky Mouse watch, yet he still he cannot be held to account. 'Wallpaper Gate', 'Covid Party Gate' – WE have elected a charlatan to run OUR beautiful county but, like our cousins across the pond, we have not got the moral guts to kick either man out of office.

No one in this totally-screwed upside-down world is held responsible for errors. From the Social Services who ignore pleas from people that a child is being molested …then killed.. yet no one is held to account. Instead they shuffled to some other Dept… and promoted just to keep things sweet - to the man we elect as the Leader of OUR country.

This book, as difficult it may be to swallow, contains a chapter on why this has come to pass. The Lefties rule with commonsense shit-canned and sent in a handbasket to Hell…at the expense of your hard-earned taxes too…

So…

…a BIG welcome guys and gals. Fasten your seat belts for I am about to take you on a journey; not altogether a pleasant one to be sure, but a road trip into the minds of some of the most mentally unstable and twisted criminal psychopaths in the UK's history.

Like all journeys there has to be a starting point, so here we are at perhaps one of the most famous, some say infamous, high security mental hospitals in Great Britain – it being Broadmoor, of course it is. Set deep into the County of Berkshire is the village of Crowthorne. It is a typical English village to be sure…with its high street, post office, a couple of public houses, barber's and a cluster of other shops, but some say that Crowthorne hides a dark history dating back to the mid 1880's.

With one-hundred-and thirty hectares of what was bleak moorland, in 1883 works began on a psychiatric hospital. Designed by Sir Joshua Jebb, KCB (1793-1863) he was a Royal Engineer and the British Surveyor-General of convict prisons. He had participated in the Battle of Plattsburg on Lake Champlain during the war of 1812; had surveyed a route between Ottawa River and Kingston where Lake Ontario flows into Saint Lawrence River, however amongst his many other notable achievements this distinguished looking man was involved in designing prisons and related buildings. Therefore, you can believe it when I say this was certainly the guy to build a secure mental asylum for he also designed Pentonville Prison in London, Woking Convict Invalid Prison and Mountjoy Prison in Belfast, added to which he knew a lot about sieges and wrote quite a few major works: *A Practical Treatise on Strengthening and Defending Outposts, Villages, Houses, Bridges, Chatham* (1836); *Modern Prisons: their Construction and Ventilation*, with plates, London (1844), and *Notes on the Theory and Practice of Sinking Artesian Wells* (1844).

Next came the somewhat longwinded titled *Manual for the Militia, of Fighting made Easy: a Practical Treatise on Strengthening and Defending*

Military Posts in reference to the Duties of a Force engaged in Disputing the Advance of an Enemy, London, 1853), and if one could wade through that lot you would not have been disappointed to get one's hands on a copy of, *A Flying Shot at Fergusson and his "Perils of Portsmouth, Invasion of England,"* pamphlet, London (1953).

Whether any military generals or admirals read these published works is unknown, but if they had had their wits about them they would have surely known all about the content of, *A practical treatise on the Duties to be performed...at a siege*, 3rd Edition, London, William Clowes and Son, 1860, London, or, *Observations on the Defence of London, with Suggestions respecting necessary Works, London*, (1860). Nevertheless his, *Reports and Observations on the Discipline and Management of Convict Prisons*, edited by the Earl of Chichester, London (1863) was a must-read for anyone with convict supervision in mind, so, without doubt Sir Joshua was the go-to guy when someone cooked up the idea to build a place to house the seriously bouncing off-the-wall, as mad as a hatters, stark raving bonkers insane. I mean he had all the experience, right? He knew how to keep people inside a building, keep other people out of a building, micro-manage anyone within and fight off anyone trying to enter the building from without or stopping anyone exiting. He was into digging artesian wells to extract the groundwater for bathing and drinking, moreover, even how to ventilate the places so everyone could breathe. C'mon guys let's give Sir Joshua a 'First Prize', and as for the Woking Convict Invalid Prison, its history makes for a fascinating read and can be found on Wikipedia.

Straying a little but from his usual construction works, the original design for Broadmoor was more of a contemporary medical building rather than a prison *per se*. The prevailing Victorian attitude was one of strict moral rectitude heavily laced with a lot of Bible thumping, furthermore the approach to mental health was one of locking people away so as not to be seen nor heard of – often ever again – and to be left with their keepers well out of harm's way.

Of note, one of the earliest asylums was 'Bethlem' in Beckenham, London. This place dates back to 1247 as a priory then opened in 1330 as a hospital. 'In every society there are those tortured by their own mind – individuals born mentally ill or afflicted by mental illness after suffering a grave misfortune', as Steven Casale writes in *Huffpost* March 2016, adding, '…but there was once an insane asylum so notorious that its very name entered the English language as words for 'chaos', 'mayhem' and 'confusion'.' Casale is, of course, referring to Bethlem Royal Hospital aka 'Bedlam', and the more one studies the histories of these 'nut houses' the more fascinating it becomes and we haven't even started meeting some of Broadmoor's murderous crackpots yet - so enjoy the trip.

But I digress for Bethlem is Europe's oldest center devoted solely to the treatment of up-the-wall, off-the fucking wall, slates missing from one's roof, stark-raving seriously mind-blowing mental upsets. Founded in 1247, the place was designed and built by Bishop Goffredo de Perfetti, an Italian, and for some Godforsaken reason he built it directly atop a sewer that frequently overflowed. Originally serving as a sanctuary for the insane it also helped to raise money for the Crusades *via* alms collection. It was not uncommon for monks and other religious figures to take in the indigent, who were often mentally ill, but one kind of smells a rat here – well it was built over a sewer of all places – because here we find our Goffredo siphoning of alms intended to help those with loose screws to financially back the Crusaders in their own series of religious wars initiated, supported, and sometimes directed by the

Latin Church in those medieval times. 'Bedlam', well that name came about from the locals who ranted and raved, muttered and moaned that it was 'bedlam *out* there and *in* there' probably on account of the racket these insane people yet despite even more protests no one could them up!

Now comes some interesting stuff because the etymology of 'asylum' started off with the Greek 'a' = 'without' coupled with 'sulon' = 'right of seizure', to become 'asulos' then 'asulon', thence to Latin with 'asylum' = 'place of refuge'. If you are one for nitpicking try late Middle English (in the sense 'place of refuge', especially for criminals) via Latin from Greek *'asulon* 'refuge, from *asulos* 'inviolable', from a – 'without' + *sulon* 'right of seizure'. So now if you want to figure that all out and if you can't – which wouldn't surprise you – please go and see a psychiatrist because I, probably no shrink, will have a clue either!

Generally speaking the people who suffered from mental illnesses were either already confined in an asylum or compassionately cared for by the families at home, however, it appears too that those unfortunates were too far gone, so-to-speak: these being 'The Unwashed Unmanageable' were kicked out onto the streets and started begging, stealing and sleeping rough, and it was during a debate in Parliament about this social problem that a solution was desired, not only to ease the street problem but also the overcrowding in already crammed places of refuge.

'As the 19th Century wore on, the local asylums became extremely reluctant to take criminal lunatics at all; they were unwelcomed in the prisons as well because they disturbed other prisoners.'

Dr Harvey Gordon: Consultant psychiatrist at Broadmoor, author of

Broadmoor.

Broadmoor's buildings were built south facing to take in vast areas of the then moorland, all designed to give the 'patients' nice views which it was thought would help with their rehabilitation.

I like to give simple analogies. so imagine if you will, taking yourself and your brood on a holiday to Spain; to learn upon unpacking your bags and to your utter dismay that your room having been advertised as having a splendid view across a sparkling azure Mediterranean Sea, has, in truth, a first-rate view of the back of a half-finished Costa del Sol hotel which seems to be either under construction or being demolished - or both at the same time. Stress, of course you would be stressed, so the relief of stress is what our indefatigable Sir Joshua Jebb had in mind when he and some cronies stood in the middle of this vast expanse of moor, pencil and paper in mind, thought for a few moments and said, 'Ah, I've got it, by Jove chaps I have it. Let's, build it facing south.' Whether or not Sir Josh ever went to the Costa del Sol could amount to a matter for heated conjecture. Nevertheless, the asylum started off with three main erections to house the men. 'Erections', you might reasonably ask? And here's another thing of some interest. Male patients in mental hospitals don't have erection because the staff put something in the tea ☺.

Oh, and smaller building providing beds for the unhinged fairer sex was included in this Grand Plan.

In later works another two blocks were added to accommodate more men, and it were the convicts from Reading Gaol who were gainfully employed with its construction which now gives the true meaning to: 'There is no such thing as a free bowl of porridge!'

It almost goes with saying that a ten-foot wall around the place was a necessary requirement, with add-ones including outer buildings of red brick and an impressive gate. Windows were, of course barred, two imposing towers with an Edward John Dent clock between them, and who better that Ed Dent to make this timepiece for in 1814 he had been given the honour of making the first Standard Astronomical Clock for the Admiralty. In 1871, Dent made the Standard Clock at the Royal Observatory, Greenwich; and in a timely fashion also making the Observatory's secondary Standard Clock, responsible for sending the signal for the emission of the six BBC pips, first broadcast in 1924. Without doubt, Edward Dent made exceedingly good clocks.

There was a school; in the ground's trees, shrubs, flowerbeds and all manner of vegetables were planted in a vast kitchen garden; most convivially designed to encourage the soon to arrive patients the opportunity to venture out into the fresh air or to save the authorities the cost of feeding them. Rhubarb was aplenty for it was regarded as a remedy for many mental ills. Nevertheless, although the hospital was opened in 1863, the prisoners who built the place remained for a further two years as they finished constructing buildings, access roads and finishing off the grand gatehouse. An avenue of trees lined a 770-metre road that gave one the impression you were in idyllic countryside. To the north of the perimeter wall were 57 staff cottages; a long two-storey brick building in the style of the main hospital sat to the south overlooking the grounds - this being the superintendent's residence. The lawns, divided by paths, were flat, ideal for bowls of croquet, and a flight of steps connected different levels the terraces divided by brick walls.

The women were to have a separate enclosed garden with a curved boundary along with an octagonal wooden shelter giving them a southwest view, and both sexes although separated could meet once a week being encouraged to join in for dance nights, perhaps a bit of 'titty-feeling' or a hand job in an adjacent broom cupboard came with the ticket. Gosh, it almost seems rather idyllic, does it not? Almost as if it were a bonus to be crackers and remember that all of these amenities were totally FREE!

Along with their escorts, among the first eight women to arrive in two horse drawn coaches on 27 May 1863, was Mary Ann Parr; a single labourer from Nottingham who'd smothered her newborn baby. Sara Allen. a Chelsea housewife, had thrown her three boys into the Thames. More stories about these patients appear in *Broadmoor Revealed: Victorian Crime and the Lunatic Asylum*, written by senior county archivist, Mark Stevens.

The first medical superintendent was John Meyer. His assistant, William Orange CNB, MD, FRCP, LSA, succeeded. Orange established 'a management style that was greatly admired'. He also advised the Home Office on how to approach criminal insanity.

From its opening, until 1948, Broadmoor was managed by a Board of Supervision, appointed by and reporting to the Home Secretary. Thereafter, the Criminal Justice Act of 1948 transferred ownership of the hospital to the Department Health (and the newly-formed NHS, and oversight to the Board of Control for Lunacy and Mental Deficiency established unto the Mental Deficiency Act 1913, which also renamed the Hospital Broadmoor Institution, which remained under the direct control of the Department of Health – a situation that reportedly 'combined notional control with actual neglect – until the establishment of the Special Hospitals Service Authority in 1989, with Charles Kaye as its first chief executive and at this point the rot started to sink in.

'…he put it about a bit…'
NHS report on Alan Franey, which details 11 allegations of sexual abuse, six of them involving patients.

There is no smoke without fire and Alan Franey ran the hospital from 1989 to 1997, having being recommended for this post – and get this – by none other than by his very close friend and serial paedophile Jimmy Savile. They had met at Leeds General Infirmary where Savile was also committing sex offences. Franey's leadership was undermined by persistent rumours of sexual impropriety and 'inappropriate activities'. Allegedly he ignored at three sexual assaults that he'd been informed about.

Back in those early days, a superintendent was in charge, with his doctors in long white coats, the nursing staff with white flowing hats; the warders dressed in black uniforms with peaked caps. And, how things developed through the years from the belief rhubarb helped mental wellbeing to electroconvulsive therapy to that strange Victorian fashion of self-electrification said to cure memory loss in more severe cases, to the milder, gentler electro-therapy called 'transcranial direct current stimulation' or tDCS that involved passing a much smaller current through the scalp to 'gently tickle the neurons underneath'. These were enlivening times to be sure and probably the main reason that many dribbling and incontinent patients were to be found wandering half-dressed around the grounds with glazed expressions, having not a clue as to who they were or where they had been minutes earlier or going to be minutes thereafter. Perhaps worse still, if one perchance was gay then ECT was used as a treatment for that too because psychiatrists back then considered homosexuality to be a mental illness. As for the application of leeches to the genitals of the more priapic males, that might be true or it might not! Yes, of course the Victorian shrinks were well-meaning enough and they sincerely believed they were trying to help the mentally sick, however, this was a traumatizing experience for people who didn't even know what planet they lived on and these practices did not last, in part because there was evidence that electricizing a person in an effort to make his stand on end signally *failed* to alter anyone's sexuality anyway.

Drugs ranging from Chlorpromazine (Largactil) to treat the symptoms of schizophrenia and other psychotic disorders, to Temazepam, both issued with consent, some without, the latter often giving paradoxical reactions of what might have been desired: those suffering from insomnia couldn't sleep for weeks, mental aggressives ran amok; hallucinations got worse; extroversion went ballistic rages intensified, thus over time the facility's walls have grown taller for very good reasons; these with a large fence erected with lights illuminating vast areas of the grounds at night. There are lots and lots of lights surrounding Broadmoor, and some people - mainly those in the incarcerated know - say that they have visited Mars and they have seen Broadmoor from there. Funny-bunny old world we live in. Right?

Back awhile, At 10am on Monday mornings thirteen satellite two-tone air raid type sirens sounded for two minutes throughout parts of Berkshire. This was followed by a continuous siren all of which the locals became accustomed to and then ignored with them only getting a tad concerned if the sirens sounded on any other day of the week to warn folk that someone had escaped. But the question arises: what *if* someone escaped on a Monday because *if* that had happened no one of course would have taken a blind bit of notice? Whether or not the patients twigged onto this slight slipup in security we will never know – probably not as most of them could not even tell the time of day, let alone which millennium it was.

Throughout the decades, the category of patients held behind Broadmoor's grim walls have become more diverse, but they are confined for a *very good* reason: they are extremely dangerous people, not only to the public but to themselves and to the staff who are charged with caring for them.

Many of the names are all too familiar to us; Kenneth Erskine aka 'The Stockwell Strangler'; Peter Sutcliffe aka 'The Yorkshire Ripper', yet there is the famous Victorian Painter, Richard Dadd (1817-1886); Edward Oxford (1822-1900) who shot at the four-month pregnant Queen Victoria on 10 June 1840. The American Army surgeon, William Chester Minor (1834-1920), the killer of one George Merrett became one of the largest contributors to the *Oxford English Dictionary* while behind Broadmoor's walls, and Christiana Edmunds aka 'The Chocolate Cream Poisoner' who struck fear through Brighton in 1871. Then we have the deluded Catherine Jones, a Welsh-speaking farmer's wife who became convinced of her own destitution and destroyed her youngest child; Miguel Vzquierdo, a Spanish terrorist whose life was spared by the villagers of the boy he killed. Royal Navy pensioner, the black William Brown whose son would go on to become a political radical and marry a suffragette.

The reason why William Chester Minor was admitted to Broadmoor was no minor matter at all. Slowly he mental condition deteriorated and, in 1902, due to delusions that he was being abducted nightly from his rooms and taken to places as far away as Istanbul and forced to commit sexual assaults on children, he cut off his own penis using the knife he had used in his work on the dictionary. Once a dickhead, no longer a dickhead, a schizophrenic, he died in Hartford, Connecticut after being moved to the 'Retreat for the Elderly Insane', in 1919.

Nevertheless, whatever good or bad that follows in this book, best we not forget these doctors and nurses so we applaud them, oh yes, I do. When co-author Christopher Berry-Dee visited Ronnie Kray and mass killer Paul

Beecham he felt that the security was a fraction that of the many US Super Max and Russian prisons he had entered over the years. Since *our* Chris – who spends most of life trying desperately to get into prisons while those inside are trying to break out – visited Broadmoor, they have upped the ante: visitors and staff are subjected to almost forensic searches and the list of banned items is extensive. How different this is to the Home Office Estate and privately sector-run prisons these days which are awash with drugs and contraband and where murderous scum such as serial sex killers have to be addressed as 'Mr' or 'Sir'. In the US 'Correctional Facilities' it is all about: 'Hey, asshole, press ya nose against the FUCKIN' WALL, and don't ya'll dare fuckin' eyeball me, ya asswipe!' Yes, my co-author Christopher… well to prove to you what I have just penned/typed above, visit his website at www.christopherberrydee.com. Look at who his con-pals are. Bless my writing buddy, simple chap he is…the only Christmas cards he gets, if any, are from people behind bars and he don't know any better!

Nevertheless, in more recent years, a multi-million-pound development was undertaken, the older buildings closed as being '…no longer fit for purpose' and put up for sale. West London NHS Trust says that the new £250 million site 'epitomises hope and recovery and would help it provide care in an environment fit for the 21st Century'. A gleaming glass façade along with new brick and concrete and a new entrance has been thrown in to house up to 210 men. Even new walls were built round the pathways, and the old siren warning system is no longer in use with just one that will sound in the grounds if something goes amiss. I've got a doorbell as loud as that because, as Chris says, I am f*****g deaf. But other than that, nothing much has really changed in the local and surrounding areas. If a patient does manage to scarper, leg it, go on his 'Bromley by Bows' or perhaps his Marilyn Monroe's, schools will go into lockdown; 'pots and pan' will collect their 'tin lids'. because those who have escaped had been known to frequent local shops - on one occasion holding a couple hostage in their own home.

With that levity done and dusted, nothing as in a BIG zilch, can ever erase the darker side of Broadmoor's history all hidden from the public gaze: suicides, patients attacking, raping sometimes murdering other patients. Patients assaulting staff; escapes. and the stories of what made these high dangerous psychopaths and lunatics tick. Even worse - The Home Office once allowed perhaps the worst serial sexually-inclined paraphiliac paedophile this country has ever known to *run* Broadmoor – Sir Jimmy Savile, indeed. And, yes, a chapter on this disgusting issue is included in this book. And, yes, this is precisely why this book is too, let's say 'non-PC': that my initial publishers got cold feet and cancelled the commission. For reasons I cannot say, there proved to be a direct linkage between Savile, press agent Max Clifford, leading government figures and BBC TV personalities leading a bit too close for comfort, if you follow my drift….thus, with the attitude of 'Let the devil take the hindmost' I self-publish, warts and all.

I have digressed. These days we have a more enlightened approach to the treatment of mental illnesses – patients now spend an average of about six years inside these facilities, or the patently untreatable are sent to the 'Big Houses', i.e. the proper prisons where any chance of escape is all but reduced to zero. 'Rehabilitation' is now the psychiatric buzz word, whereas the Victorian attitude to the treatment of those with a few slates missing on their roofs was to lock 'em up and throw away the key, all rather Dickensian – well it had to be back then because society didn't know any better.

These days, Broadmoor High Security Hospital with his long history of caring for men and women under the Mental Health Act has a brilliant future, but as that develops we cannot ignore its past which was often deadly indeed but misquoting from that incredible Stephen King 1999 fantasy/drama *The Green Mile*: 'What happens on the moor stays on the moor'.

Period…so let's meet Christopher Brand.

***

Christopher Brand.

Born circa 1960 (the exact date is unknown) Christopher had been in and out of prison for minor offences including a few thefts since the age of sixteen and presently serving two years for burglary and traffic violations, and it has been said that he had previously spent periods in Broadmoor for self-harming.

What is known is; that during 1980 he was an inmate at HMP Woodhill, a 'Category 'A' prison in Milton Keynes, the town known for its roundabouts, straight-lined streets, odd avenue names and a 19th Century estate, where, during WWII, the Enigma Code was solved at Bletchley Park. And it was while at HMP Woodhill, Brand murdered a fellow inmate who was on remand for sexual offences and indecent assault by forcing his head under bath water. At trial, Brand was found guilty of murder and was sentenced to a minimum of twelve years. 12 years…I know people who have cats older than that! Actually, I had a dear old grey-rinsed neighbour who reckoned that her Budgie ''Billy' would have lived 12 years…but her cat ate it.

Back in the 1980s, the then equivalent of today's HM Inspectorate of Prisons regarded HMP Woodhill as 'poorly rated'. Inmate supervision was sorely lacking and at one point while being held at Woodhill in 1992, Brand inserted razor blades into his rectum in a bizarre attempt to commit suicide. However, although this may not be the subject over dinner, people who have ingested 'foreign bodies' that may become lodged in the rectum may present (suffer) – and this will come as no surprise – a pinched-face expression; rectal pain or bleeding, constipation with constipation, pruritus, a mincing gate with diffuse abdominal pain thrown in as a free gift, so quite where Brand got that idea from nobody knows.

This twenty-something young man clearly understood that something was wrong with him; for being a persistent offender, to drown someone in a bath to go onto inserting razor blades into one's own backside are not the actions of a completely healthy mind, so he was sharp enough to know that a mental assessment was a priority. He was trying to seek psychiatric help, so he demanded that the authorities send him to HMP Grendon Springhill – a Category 'D' men's prison, located in the village of Grendon Underwood, in Buckinghamshire, which has a unique history itself.

'It seems like an inside job to me!'
A detective sergeant; commenting on the April 2003 burglary at HMP Grendon Springhill.

No, no…that officer's observation did NOT, I stress DID NOT allude to Brand razoring his bowels…no, no, so please if there was some confusion here, I am referring to Grendon Under-the-Wood or is it 'Underwood?

In 1624, Grendon Underwood lay on forest tracks used gypsies and strolling players) travelling performers) and was visited more than once by William Shakespeare, who stayed at the house, formerly an inn, now known as 'Shakespeare House' now a 5 Star guest house. Indeed, The *Domesday Book* of 1086 records the village as 'Grennnedone'…and…here's the thing, instead while watching too much crap soap on TV, one sits ignorant of the richly, illuminating history of our nation…something that our children should/must be taught at schools. Hey, guys and gals, in 1086 American had not even been invented let alone patented, and it took us Brits to land at Cape Cod, Massachusetts, circa November 1620, to start what they thought was a colony, which turned into a republic to be turned into the totally fucked-up nation that it is today…courtesy Donald Trump.

Built as a family home in 1872, originally known as Grendon Hall, during WWII the site was initially used as a base for MI6 and a training centre for the Special Operations Executive, so one expects that Ian Fleming aka James Bond, knew about the place. It first opened its doors in 1953, as a secure Home Office psychiatric unit to treat antisocial personality disorders; it was also the first 'Open Prison' in the UK. Furthermore, it was so 'open' that in 2003 it became the first prison ever to be burgled. I kid you not, Former inmates had cased the place then stole £650 from a safe and made off with a bag of swag which included personal effects, including mobile phones from the inmate's lockers. So, one could not make that one up if one tried! However, any expectations Brand had about being transferred to a more cushy 'nick' were short-lived for he was a Category 'A' prisoner and sending him to an open prison where inmates could literally wander around the expansive grounds at will with some of those who had been released returning to burgle the place, was the last thing the Home Office's had on its collectively pen-pushing mind!

Although initially being given a twelve-year stretch, Brand had, by now, served twenty-two years, so it was now that he took a stand. He went on hunger strike. Refusing food for seventeen days in protest at the conditions, he was thrown into a cell previously home to an inmate who had made a 'dirty protest' and had defecated and urinated over the floor the walls, even the bedding.

Usually when an inmate carries out a 'dirty protest' he is ordered to clean the mess up, and for this he is rewarded a few points, but Brand was made of sterner stuff. There was no way he was going to clean up someone else's dirt. He told the governor that to do so was contrary to Health & Safety rules and regulations, against the European Convention of Human Rights 'Article 3'. Therefore, although staging a hunger strike would achieve little after seventeen days in 'The Hole', it is believed that the prison governor, now caught between a rock and a hard place reluctantly showed concern and came to the conclusion that he wanted Robert well out of his prison and shipped off someplace else.

Broadmoor, here we come!

At this time Broadmoor was divided into two houses with various ward names - one being single storey 'Bedford House; with windows looking over gardens east of the main entrance and next to the outer wall. Built in 1980, it was spacious, clean, the doors with toughened glass and not the straight corridors with barred windows. As one former employee said: 'It was like going from analogue to digital', when compared to the old red brick 'eruptions' with their long dark corridors and green-painted doors. And, it was at 'Bedford House' where Christopher Brand was bedded in Luton Ward.

As an aside…what is it about Luton which makes its placename an ideal ward name for people who are as off-the-wall, up-the-friggin'- wall as one can be? Why not something more subtle? Let's say 'Bognor Regis Ward' for example because at least Bognor has some water close by. Why not 'Seychelles Ward'? Give me a break will ya'll. Where is some 'inspiration' here?

Nonetheless, Luton Ward was a secure unit where all 'patients' who first enter Broadmoor are assessed; therefore, this period of adjustment can be difficult and traumatic. Doors are locked. Rooms placed under 24-hour watch; these are of course highly regulated and structured days and, like all hospitals, set mealtimes – nothing fancy, just standard hospital food (which as we know is pretty crap at the best of times), and why not, say's me? Try Butlins at Bognor Regis and you'll understand why. Therefore any misconceptions that a Broadmoor patient gets steak and chips with all the trimmings is far from the truth. Well, maybe not as we shall see later when we meet Peter Sutcliffe aka 'The Yorkshire Ripper'.

So Brand now finds himself in an extremely restricted environment. Only plastic cutlery and plates, lukewarm drinks served in plastic cups, and there can be nothing more unappetizing than warm toast washed down with tepid tea with any complaints always falling on deaf ears. So if any readers have ideas about going insane, we would suggest that you think again!

For Brand, just like any other patient, time spent on any ward varies depending on one's capacity to 'accept the treatment'. Psychiatric staff try to build up a picture of a person's state of mind. Nothing is left to chance for these men are some of the most dangerous and unpredictable individuals in the UK, and Brand is now considered amongst them. No one escapes from this part of the hospital, an area that will hopefully shape his, and everyone else's treatment and in some cases one's path out of the 'system'. It used to be believed that once a person entered Broadmoor it was very difficult to be moved onto new horizons, but patients have to be willing …'to accept, adapt and integrate.. It's a two-way street: Broadmoor *allegedly* has the knowledge, the tools and plenty of time. For some who enter those gates there will be no release - Christopher Brand has become one of them.

Settled into the unit, Brand was kept under watch by nurses who peeked through a plastic type of porthole, scratched and barely see-through ,each observation noted in a log. The corridors were long, with an 'L-shape' leading to a nursing station. The paintwork smelled fresh, toughened windows giving views to the outside. Brand – as are all of his peers – was assigned as a 'Key Worker' which gave him all of the information he needed during this settling down period. He could wear his own clothes and shoes – even belts back then when things were more lax. Yet, somehow in 2013, Brand obtained a pair of spectacles and from where he got them no one knows.

With an hourly watch over him, at some point - and there is an optical point to this - Brand snapped one arm of the glasses off and it was not until a nurse heard him moaning and groaning then peered through the small observation widow and entered did staff note that he'd forced the sharp end into the head of his penis – as in OUCH!

Well, didn't I explain earlier that this book is not for the faint-hearted, did I not? Nevertheless, lacking the surgical expertise to remove a part of a pair of spectacles from a place they were patently not designed for, Brand was whisked off to Frimley Park Hospital some four miles distant. During the next day, while under a general anesthetic a surgeon who was also wearing spectacles fiddled around a bit and removed a spectacle arm from Brand's penis, thenceforth, the totally mentally shot-to-fuck man was returned to Broadmoor with any thought of masturbating put out of his tiny mind forever.

But wait a moment, for despite being placed under even closer supervision, fifteen days later Brand did it again and once *again* no one has a clue as to where he got another pair of glasses – at least without a prescription. So, it was left to Frimley Park Hospital to do some more penile repair work, but this time the damage – as one would expect – was much more severe. With that jobbie being done, after a short stay at Frimley Park a limping Brand, catheter still in place, discharged himself the following morning and returned to Broadmoor, probably vowing never to do it again.

So why would Brand do such a stupid thing? Well, there are two schools of thought with some saying that he simply wanted to have a day out and see something new, as in meeting different people in different surroundings. Others say that it was his way of crying for help. So, I have come up with this scenario: he achieved both.

(1)   Brand certainly had two days out of Broadmoor and went somewhere different and where he met different people and a surgeon who wore spectacles.

(2)   Brand certainly winced a lot and wouldn't anyone under these rather shortsighted circumstances?

Indeed, it has been said that he also snapped the catheter while in situ, but this can't be verified at the time of writing and who really cares anyway? Nonetheless, here we have Mr Brand once again placed in a seclusion room and watched like a proverbial hawk. He was issued with a cocktail of drugs to alleviate the pain he was well-deservedly suffering; Tramadol, being a strong painkiller used to block 'signals' from travelling along the nerves, or something along those lines without getting too technical, and Pregabalin which is used to treat epilepsy. Oh, and I almost forgot the Zopiclone – a sleeping tablet which, under normal circumstances, takes about one hour to take effect.

Moving swiftly on, hospital records show that on Monday, 1 July 2013, the door to Brand's room was opened as normal at 7.15am, and it is claimed that none of the nursing staff had checked him during the night shift. Whether or not this was the case seems to matter little for if anyone had looked through the peephole, all they would have noticed was their patient apparently fast asleep anyway. Nevertheless, according to the coroner's report, ten minutes passed before staff found Brand unresponsive and efforts to resuscitate him failed. As Brand's demise could not be put down to "Cause of Death – Natural", the police were informed, and it was further noticed by a nurse that there was a plastic cup with a pink residue in its base, so would any of the drugs, or any combination of these drugs, leave a pink residue? Your principal author, Boris, says 'probably no,' simply because all of the medication Brand took was prescribed as above It was allegedly highly controlled with nothing else issued. However, this being an unnatural death, police forensic experts concluded that the pink substance was an anti-depressant – something for which Brand received no such medication. Therefore, I have to conclude that he obtained, by hook or by crook, the anti-depressants from another patient, and when mixed with his prescribed drugs made up the lethal cocktail that killed him.

And, it is at this point that things get very messy, indeed they do to, for the inquest and coroner's report carried out between 11 and 12 April 2016 – nearly three years after Brand's death – concluded that Brand died of 'Natural Causes', when this was patently untrue for it was suicide while the balance of the mind was disturbed, and there is no doubt about that all. Furthermore, further study of the coroner's report draws us to confusion about dates and times too. It claims that Brand's door was unlocked at 7.15am on Wednesday, 1 July 2015 when in fact it *was* 1 Monday, July 2013. In 'Section 3 of the Matters', the coroner wrote that there was a delay in the CPR evidence which showed that the it was the fourth person , not the first member of staff who entered Brand's room who commenced resuscitation, thus not as the records would have us believe. Indeed, Coroner Peter Bedford didn't mince his words when he wrote: '…urgent action is needed to prevent further deaths at your hospital and your organisation has the power to do it.'

Brand was fifty-three-years old when he killed himself. Sadly, nothing much is known about his life's narrative other than what is revealed here. We know nothing either about his parents, his schooling, if he had siblings, whether he had a good upbringing or not can help us to try and understand how and why he turned to petty crime and went mentally downhill faster that an Olympic skier soon after.

The basic reasons for self-harming in itself is readily understood, and if we try to retro-construct an individual's narrative this can give us a few clues; one being that Brand may have suffered some form of physical or sexual abuse as a youngster, most certainly relationship problems with family and relations would be included here. Criminologist, Christopher Berry-Dee, has spent several decades interviewing sadosexual serial killers, and self-harming is a very rare phenomena amongst that murderous breed with them needing to harm others and *not* themselves. And yet another reason for self-harming is being unemployed or having difficulties at work, as The Royal College of Psychiatrists will readily agree, in more simplistic terms an innate issue of feeling bad about oneself.

Another reason people self-harm is the feeling that people are not listening to oneself. There is a feeling of helplessness and hopelessness, of isolation; almost if one is out-of-control, the sense that one is powerless, that all one does there is nothing one can do to change anything. It is that caught between a rock and a hard place scenario, and it is a very sad place for *anyone* to be. The ironic thing is that self-harming is more likely to occur if one is being prescribed a cocktail of drugs to suppress the desire to self-harm. Suppression is *not* a cure and there can be no arguing with that! Of course, most people suffer in silence, yet in Brand's case I feel that he consciously wanted to show others how distressed he was, and he wanted to get back at them, to punish them for not listening to him.

Yes, he had murdered another inmate; indeed to the Home Office he'd became almost unmanageable, a pain in the correctional system's backside, so at their wits end he was shipped off to Broadmoor. It's for the reader to judge whether one thinks that Christopher Brand was evil. He was clinically insane either despite the fact that here we find him dumped in Broadmoor simply because there was no place else to put him.

Christopher Berry-Dee vividly recalls the words of Connecticut serial killer, the now executed Michael Bruce Ross (1959-2005) who said to him during a television interview on Death Row, Somers Connecticut:

Ya, know Chris. Sometimes I wanted so much to clear my head. I tried so hard. I felt that I was like a spider trying to climb up a pane of glass, almost reaching the top only to fall down again and again. Then they prescribed me drugs and it only made matters worse for me. As soon as the drugs wore off…it was like living with an obnoxious neighbor in my head who kept intruding over and over. I am not afraid of dying. It's just that I don't want to be around when it happens.

Perhaps Christopher Brand felt a similar way about his life for he fell asleep, not conscious, thus not around, when his end happened either. I do not try to mitigate Brand's criminal behaviour: life is for living and for dying. It is the way it is!

***

William 'Bill' Giles - by Raychel Andrews.

During the 1880's, in an era when bleeding and purging were used as treatments to tackle mental illnesses, children could be sent to Broadmoor from aged seven-years-old: then the age of criminal responsibility.

A particularly disturbing tale involved perhaps Broadmoor's longest-serving patient, Bill Giles, who was merely 10-years-old when he entered the asylum in 1885. His so-called offence was that of setting fire to three bales of hay. Declared to be an 'imbecile' who was also prone to psychosis, he spent seventy-seven years behind the grim walls, dying there in March 1962 at the age of 87.

Note: a particularly interesting article where William Giles is mentioned is API PARLIAMENT UK *'TRANSFER OF BROADMOOR PATIENTS'* (HANSARD, 15 MARCH 1962 VOL 238 CC305.)

'The Cutlass-wielding Captain', by Raychel Andrews.

George Johnson was certainly no fictional character from the movie series *Pirates of the Caribbean*, for he was the real-life captain of the *Tory*, a 382-ton barge built at Yarmouth in 1834 and acquired by the New Zealand Company. It is erroneously claimed that in 1845 *Tory* was on passage from Hong Kong to Liverpool when thirty-six-year-old Captain Johnson killed one of his crew with a bayonet in a drunken rage. This date is incorrect. As a matter of fact, an examination of the Tory's log shows that she was one of three New Zealand Company surveyor ships sent off in haste to prepare for settlers in New Zealand. She dropped anchor in Queen Charlotte Sound on 17 September 1839 to pick up fresh water, food and timber before proceeding to Port Nicholson on 20 September.

Tory struck a sandbank at the entrance to Kaipara Harbour. She was repaired and left Port Nicholson for Sydney on 19 April 1840 where she was refitted. In an effort to gain cargo she first sailed to Surabaya and then Batavia. Eventually at Singapore she obtained cargo for Macao. The *Tory* was wrecked in the Palawan Passage, Philippines, on 23 January 1841.

Nonetheless, Capt. Johnson tried to excuse his actions by claiming he was quelling a mutiny. However, his crew testified that their skipper 'was in a continual excitement from drink' and 'amused himself by ordering men into irons and cutting them with a sabre'. Capt. Johnson was subsequently found 'Not Guilty' at the Old Bailey on the grounds of insanity and sent to Bethlam. In 1864 he was given a bed at Broadmoor, where he worked mainly in the kitchen garden, but it is said that he suffered forever with delusions of persecution. Nonetheless, his wife continually petitioned the Home Secretary for his discharge, which was finally granted in 1868. Indeed, he wrote a book with the somewhat longwinded title: *The life of Captain Johnson, late captain of the ship 'Tory', with his statement of the circumstances of his last voyage; together with observations containing facts in refutation of the various charges brought against him.*

Well, done, George!

***

Peter Bryan.

> '…out of the frying pan and into the fire.'
>
> J.R.R. Tolkien (1892-1973).

One looks at a frying pan and knows exactly what it's intended for – to fry something in such as eggs and bacon, perhaps part of someone's brain as evidenced by Dr Hannibal Lecter eating parts of Ray Liotta's grey matter in that 2001 movie. However for a few folks the frying pan has a more sinister application. Peter Bryan was one of them and he *was* Broadmoor sinister indeed!

Born in London in 1968; the youngest of seven siblings of an immigrant from Barbados, Peter attended schools in Forest Gate then Canning Town. It comes down to us that his formative years were normal enough, nothing remarkable either way and that he finished his education at the somewhat early age of fourteen. Gaining employment at a local market clothes stall, the rag trade seems like a family interest as later work took him along the same route, furthermore, Bryan was often seen at local soup kitchens teaching people how to cook – a portent for things to come, maybe? Yet this work did provide an income for Bryan, and he lived in a nearby doss house called 'The Flying Angel', a former seamen's mission just one-hundred-yards from Freemasons Road, Newham, which upon one side was Custom House the other being Canning Town. Rivalry between the two sides of Freemasons Road was legendary until it came to football with West Ham uniting them during match time and resuming to fisticuffs and territorial disputes starting over again and thereafter.

Back then this locality was a docker's area; a place where foreign seaman would stay with the locals who also robbed them while in the drink. So unsafe it was, the local kids ran errands for a few shillings for the seamen who were too scared to leave their ships. Of some note, 'The Flying Angel' was a Victorian eight-floor building, big enough to accommodate up to three hundred merchant seamen, soon to be converted into a home for the mentally unstable: a place for refuge, food and general help, and directly opposite Custom House light railway station - all-in-all a rough area with the world-famous Repton boxing club just down the street.

It is now 1987. Bryan is eighteen and for some reason the youth made his way up to the sixth floor of 'The Flying Angel', walked into one of the rooms and set about a man in an unprovoked attack during which Bryan tried to throw his victim out of a window. The man made his escape leaving Bryan with a deep cut to his head, the police were called and after a talk with both men the case was dropped with no further action was taken.

Now persona non grata at his lodgings, Bryan found a flat at Derby Street, Forest Gate, East London. At the Sheth's family run clothing business on the Kings Road, Chelsea, he was given a job and soon took a fancy to Seth's daughter, twenty-year-old Nisha. He harassed her and then repaid his boss by stealing clothes from him. He was sacked. A week later on Thursday, 18 March 1993, Bryan, now aged twenty-three, returned to the premises with a claw hammer and began to beat Nisha around the head and body as she chatted on the telephone. He killed her right in front of her twelve-year-old brother, Bobby, who, in a brave attempt to shield his sister, now lives with this mental trauma and possibly will do so for the remainder of his life.

Whether or not Bryan felt some remorse for this killing we don't know, but high on cannabis he soon attempted suicide by jumping off of a third-floor balcony of a building in Battersea, succeeding in merely breaking both legs – perhaps, as time would soon testify, it might have been a lot better for everyone if he'd landed on his head instead of his feet. Nonetheless, Bryan went to trial, pled guilty to manslaughter on the grounds of diminished responsibility: an unbalanced mental state of mind that is considered to make a person less answerable for a crime and to be grounds for a reduced charge, not always of course classifying them as insane, he was packed off to Rampton High Security Hospital, near the village of Woodbeck.

Bryan stayed at Rampton for eight years. He was regarded as a 'model patient who has made considerable progress,' then in 2001 he was moved to a low security unit called 'Riverside House' in Seven Sisters, a sub-district of Tottenham, north London.

The slack regime at this 'low support' hostel was such that every patient had keys to their rooms *and* the front door, so they could more-or-less come and go as they pleased. In January 2004, Bryan's mental health and social worker wrote to the Home Office stating that he was '…no longer a person of concern and no risk to the public.' Oops, and what a mistake that was too, for although he was granted his freedom, soon enough he was in trouble again. A sixteen-year-old (some say she was 17) girl alleged that he had sexually assaulted her very close to the hostel in Seven Sisters Road. Deny it he couldn't for he was actually caught 'blowing raspberries on her stomach.' Her family made threats to the authorities and Bryan was placed in Newham General Hospital's psychiatric 'Topaz' ward for his own safety. Then, after a relatively short stay, he went and bought a claw hammer, a Stanley knife and a screwdriver.

Living alone in a ground floor flat at 1. Manning House, The Drive, Walthamstow, east London Described as a 'nice man', aged forty-three, Brian Cherry, small in build, about 5ft 7ins tall with brown hair and a straggly beard, had known Bryan for some years, and during the evening of Tuesday, 17 February 2004, he invited Bryan around for dinner. Oh gosh, if only Cherry had known what his pal wanted to eat, then the invitation would have been withdrawn *toot suite*.

At some point during the evening, neighbours heard banging noises and a close friend of the amiable Cherry, a Nicola Newman, let herself into the flat at around 7.15pm. Immediately she noticed a strong smell of disinfectant, and Holy shit, there, emerging from the sitting room and now standing in front of her was bare-chested Peter Bryan holding a bloodstained breadknife. 'Brian is dead', Bryan blandly said. The police arrived to find him standing in the hallway in the dark with bloodstained hands, jeans and trainers. Strewn around the place were all manner of 'weapons and tools' with a slight aroma of cooked meat also present. And there was Bryan in the kitchen - contradicting the neighbour by seeing Bryan next to the cooker tending a sizzling frying pan and using a fish slice to toss the contents around. Cherry's naked corpse lay on the carpeted floor. The arms and a leg had been sawn off.

It was also said, and there really cannot be any dispute here, that the cops noticed that Cherry's skull had been cracked open and the brain – or part thereof – removed and was in the process of being fried. Next to this was an open tub of butter. More brain tissue and hair matted with blood was heaped on a plate next to a knife and fork on the draining board.

Upon seeing the police, Bryan casually said: 'I ate his brain with butter, it was really nice.' Later he added, 'I would have done someone else if you hadn't come along…I wanted their souls', a sort of trademark off-hand remark he had used previously in the Sheth case.

At autopsy it was shown that Cherry's skull had been smashed open with at least twenty-four blows from a hammer and his head had been partly sawn off. Bryan had also hacked off his right leg and both arms. Blood was spattered around the living room and three bloodstained knives were strewn around the floor. The severed left leg was 'partly sawn and partly fractured'. At the top of the right left the muscle had been completely divided and 'superficial sawing of the bone had commenced'. Prosecutor Aftab Jafferjee said: 'The defendant had been interrupted before he could complete the amputation of that limb'.

Bryan later admitted that he was 'comforted by the smell of blood', adding: 'I used the Stanley knife to cut then off and some other kitchen knives, but I had to stamp on them to break the bone.'

Notwithstanding this, Bryan was first remanded to HMP Pentonville where he told a prison officer that he wanted to kill a warder and eat someone's nose and officers had to use riot shields when unlocking his cell in case of attack. Following his trial, he was sent HMP Belmarsh in Thamesmead southeast London, a 'Category 'A' prison housing some of the most dangerous offenders in the British Criminal Justice System. On Thursday, 15 April 2004, Bryan was sent to Broadmoor and placed in seclusion.

Worse was yet to come.

While on bail for the rape of a man in 2002, aged fifty-nine, Richard Loudwell had been diagnosed with a whole raft of mental shortcomings and been convicted of the manslaughter of eighty-two-year-old Joan Smythe, in Rainham, Kent, leaving her naked and very dead, her body covered with cigarette burns and bites. Then this halfwit dialed 999 to tell the operator that 'the lady is seriously ill and asleep'. A report identified 'a number of failings' in the lead-up to her death. Loudwell had been admitted to hospital twice in 2002 and assessed in the community twice before helping Mrs Smythe home with her shopping. To make matters worse, on the day of the old dear's murder, Loudwell's sister had telephone his probation officer to ask for help about his 'increasingly bizarre and troubled behaviour, but she received no reply. Of course, and as might be expected, not one person was held accountable. Nevertheless, in another whitewash, the independent inquiry into Loudwell's care and treatment was commissioned by Medway Council and Medway Teaching Primary Care Trust (PCT), concluding with typical pen-pushing stupidity: '…was unable to conclude that the homicide that Richard Loudwell committed was either predictable or preventable'. How banal is that, nevertheless, with that all papered over he was held at a secure unit until his trial in April 2004. Loudwell had only been in Broadmoor three days when one could say that he got his comeuppance.

At that time dining areas in Broadmoor were communal unless any of the then nineteen patients in Luton Ward were considered far too dangerous and had to eat in their rooms with food being served through a hatch, thus, it was during Sunday, 25 April 2004, that Bryan went for Loudwell in Luton Ward.

It was at 6.10pm when Bryan pounced. Using a drawstring from his tracksuit pants he tightened the cord around Loudwell's neck while repeatedly smashing the man's head on the floor. Bryan was of stocky build, a shaven head and dark ominous eyes. While there were nine staff on duty, not one of them was present in the dining area during the attack. Believe it or not the staff were taking a meal break in another room (the ICA room) situated off the dayroom, the door to which was shut. Three staff were observing the two corridors on which the patients' own rooms were located. The nearest staff were in the ward office and could only see into the dayroom but could not see into the dining room and Bryan only gave up this murderous attack because he said, 'I was exhausted'.

Sometime later he told a psychiatrist: 'I've had these urges towards him [Loudwell] for a long time [three days]. I was just waiting for my chance to get to him. He is at the bottom of the food chain, old haggard…he looked like he's had his innings…I wanted to kill him and eat him. I didn't have much time. If I did, I'd have tried to cook him and eat him.' For his part, Loudwell was rushed to hospital none the wiser as to why Bryan had flipped. He died on Saturday, 5 June 2004, from bronchopneumonia caused by severe brain injuries.

In 1.2 of the report's executive summary, it said: 'No single individual, whether patient or member of staff, was responsible for death of Richard Loudwell. There were in our view deficiencies in many aspects of the care provided to both Richard Loudwell and Peter Bryan and shortcomings at every level within the Trust. It was the combination of these shortcomings that led to Richard Loudwell's death.' So, no one, not even Peter Bryan was responsible for this homicide, a 'combination of shortcomings' was the offender, was it? Perhaps the fact *none* of Broadmoor's staff were present in the dining room might have had something to do with it, but no one was held accountable, so the buck didn't stop anywhere.

At the time of this attack on Loudwell, Bryan had been in Broadmoor for just ten days.

So what do we make of Peter Bryan? Looking back to his very early days there was absolutely nothing wayward, nothing to suggest that he would ever become a cannibal at all, yet here we find him frying the brain of a man all of which is very reminiscent of the 2001 movie *Hannibal*, where Paul Krendler, played by Ray Liotta, has had the top of his skull sawed open by Dr Hannibal Lecter, a portion from the prefrontal lobe sautéed in a frying pan with shallot and white wine.

At his 2005 Old Bailey trial for the murder of Brian Cherry and Richard Loudwell, Judge Giles Forrester said that Bryan should never be released as he gave him two life sentences. Passing sentence Judge Forrester said:

'Anyone who has listened to the chilling facts of this case
and read the material can be in no doubt that your case is

extremely grave. On the occasions when you killed you had been suffering from an abnormality of mind and that is, and remains, paranoid schizophrenia, a severe mental illness manifesting itself in unpredictable and extreme violence.

'In respect to the offences present before the court you had the urge not only to kill but also eat the flesh of your victims. In the first case you did so because for a while you were undisturbed.

'You wanted to do your voodoo, as you told doctors. By eating the flesh of your victims, you felt feelings of power and invincibility. Not only that but you derived sexual excitement from the sexual act.'

At this point in his summing up, His Honour got down to the nitty-gritty, with:

'What is of particular concern is your ability to mask your psychopathic symptoms under a veneer of normality. You are extremely dangerous. Dr Martin Lock has described you as the most dangerous man he had ever come across and the protection of the public in a case like this must come above all other considerations. You cannot be trusted in the community.'

Of some further interest is why and when did Bryan decide that he wanted to kill Loudwell? Author Christopher Berry-Dee has learned through leaked documents that Loudwell was disruptive for a while but soon settled down, however, throughout his stay at Belmarsh he was considered unsuitable to share accommodation with other prisoners. On Sunday, 5 January 2003 an attempt to allow him onto a six bedded ward in association to watch television led to him being threatened after his 'index' (the murder of the old lady) became known. On Sunday, 23 March 2003, a prison intelligence report noted that three prisoners were planning to assault him on his return from exercise. On Monday, 28 April a teacher reported that the prisoners in her class had threatened that they would kill Loudwell if he came to their ward. However, absent from any report was mention that Peter Bryan had been one of the three men who had threatened to kill Loudwell.

Getting Loudwell admitted to Broadmoor was more difficult than it might have seemed, for on Wednesday, 28 May 2003 a Specialist Registrar from Broadmoor, assessed Loudwell as requiring medium rather than maximum security. On 31 July the Broadmoor Admissions Panel refused Loudwell a bed on the basis that he was more appropriately looked after in conditions of medium security but finding such a place proved impossible, so he was bounced back to Broadmoor and, on Thursday, 20 November 2003, he was offered a bed. With that being established, shortly afterwards a medium secure unit did offer a place, but this was not accepted in the light of the offer of a place from Broadmoor. Indeed, there is some evidence that even the Home Office Mental Health Unit stuck its fingers into this mess, insisting that Loudwell go to Broadmoor.

And it was at this point that the wheels started to fall off of the wagon, for at the time of the attack on Loudwell, Bryan's assessment by his RMO (Responsible Medical Officer – lucky they are not called IMOs (Irresponsible Medical Officers) a consultant forensic psychiatrist was 'incomplete'. As far as Loudwell was concerned, a pre-admission nursing assessment was prepared by 'Nurse Consultant # 1' (name removed to protect identity) appeared to have little practical value to Broadmoor staff. In particular it failed to identify the risk that Loudwell was at from other patients, one of whom was Peter Bryan who had vowed to kill him while at HMP Belmarsh. Therefore, Loudwell was told to keep his mouth shut. But you see 'Loudmouth Loudwell' started mouthing off to other patients and it is fair to add that staff were ill-prepared to deal with his disclosures and supergluing his lips together was not an option.   In effect, he was energetically digging his own grave.

Loudwell was on a regime of constant observation for his first week on Luton Ward. Despite this he was attacked on several occasions without staff noticing. He had water and ash thrown over him. He was also subjected to spitting and verbal abuse. However, despite all of this, observations were not carried out to an appropriate standard, nor were adequate records of any observations maintained.

The long and short of this was, although Loudwell complained to staff about these attacks nothing much more could be done to protect him and any advice given to him by staff he blatantly ignored; the upshot being the failure to fully address the bullying of Loudwell and the attack by Peter Bryan on 25 April. If the bullying had been taken sufficiently seriously it is unlikely that Bryan would have had the opportunity to mount a sustained attack in the dining room without being observed by staff.

The September 2009, 437 pages *Independent inquiry into the care and treatment of Peter Bryan and Richard Loudwell* for NHS London, in part makes for grim reading, in other parts it is a damning indictment of the failings at Broadmoor at that time.

At his appeal in January 2006, Lord Chief Justice Lord Phillips, overturned the 'whole life' tariff but said it was unlikely that Bryan, who is mentally ill, would ever be released. The reason for the Court of Appeal's decision was that '…how long does justice demand that he be held in custody for crimes committed when ill?'

In conclusion the author is drawn to the remarks made by Judge Giles Forrester, and in fear of repeating this again, I do so in focusing in on: 'What is of particular concern is '…*your ability to mask your psychopathic symptoms under a veneer of normality* [author's italics]'

Christopher Berry-Dee has examined this 'mask of normality' that almost all criminal psychopaths wear and he has written extensively about this in his many internationally bestselling books. These types are controlling people who have no conscience such as we normal folk enjoy. They are also arch manipulators of this there can be no debate. But what if one links psychopathy with schizophrenia, because serial killers suffering from paranoid schizophrenia are very rare indeed? In a paper published in June 1999, *Psychopathy and Violent Behavior Among Patients with Schizophrenia or Schizoaffective Disorder*, the writer K.A. Nolen concludes:

> 'The comorbidity of schizophrenia and psychopathy was found to be higher among violent patients with schizophrenia than among non-violent patients. Violent patients with schizophrenia (which Peter Bryan had been diagnosed as suffering long before he was found a place in Broadmoor) who score high on measures of psychopathy may have a personality disorder that precedes the emergence of psychotic symptoms, or they may constitute a previously unclassified subtype of schizophrenia, characterised by early symptoms of conduct disorder symptoms and persistent violent behavior.'

described Bryan as 'the most dangerous man he had ever come across.'

When asked if wanting to eat people was normal, Peter Bryan replied: 'Of course it's normal. Cannibalism is normal. It's been here was centuries. If I was on the street, I'd go for someone bigger, you know, for the challenge.'

Referring to Richard Loudwell, Bryan said: 'I felt excited when I attacked him. I wanted to shag him when he was alive and also when he was dead. I wanted to cook him but there was no time, now was there access to cooking equipment. I briefly considered eating him raw.'

But it gets worse. Dr Martin Lock who carried out the series of 'Silence of the Lambs' style of interviews with Bryan who said: '…and you look like a brainy chap, and you are quite slim. I think I could take you.' He went on to describe the victim's arms and leg as 'tasting like chicken'.

If one is interested in cannibalism, one might read: *Cannibal Serial Killers: Profiles of Flesh-Eating Murderers* by Christopher Berry-Dee with Victoria Redstall.

No nightmares please!

***

Robert John Maudsley.

'If there ever was a cast-in-stone blueprint for creating a monster we find it writ dysfunctionally large in the formative-through-teenage years of Robert Maudsley.

In all my years studying and interviewing serial killers from around the world, the abuse meted out during young Maudsley's early years have shocked even me.'

Christopher Berry-Dee.

In a morbid kind of way or maybe not, Maudsley is one who should fascinate us all for all the right and wrong reasons too. Could it be either that Maudsley's upbringing had something to do with what happened in spawning one of the most dangerous men the British criminal justice system has ever dealt with, or a misguided even obtuse belief that he had rid us of the evil that a certain type of perverted criminal brings with him into society – meaning Maudsley's victims, that is.

The name Maudsley has Anglo-Saxon roots; all originating when a family resided in the settlement of 'Mawdesley' in the county of Lancashire, and the name seems innocuous enough, but now think to the well-known 1991 released movie, *The Silence of the Lambs*, and Dr Hannibal Lecter, and the 'Wolfman of Wakefield' are just two the of names Maudsley has been called in the past, and, of course, the fear he strikes into others still resonates with us – for even today this very British killer is housed in a cage very similar to that of our fava bean eating, Chianti sipping, Dr Lecter, except that Robert Maudsley *is real* while Lecter *is not*!

Robert Maudsley was born in the Toxteth area of Liverpool on Friday, 26 June 1953, into a lower-class working family living in Myrtle Street in the area known as the Knowledge Quarter' – a stone's throw from Liverpool Metropolitan Cathedral. The fourth child of a coal delivery driver, George, who was known as an alcoholic, a violent and abusive man. Around the age of six months, Robert, his older sister Brenda and two older brothers Kevin and Paul were placed into care as it was believed that both parents had neglected them. It was said neighbours reported hearing violent outbursts, children screaming and felt at the time help was needed for their safety.

It would be fair to say that living in a two-up-two-down overcrowded terraced house took its toll on a lot of families, moreover, Liverpool was vastly becoming more overcrowded. Nazareth House on the Liverpool Road at Crosby – now a care home – was then a local Catholic Orphanage which was staffed by the sisters of Nazareth aka the 'Poor Sisters of Nazareth' – a Catholic apostolic congregation. A three-story building set in lush grounds, from the outside it looked clean, tidy and well run with dormitories throughout. Once through a gate, a short drive leads up to the entrance of a vast Grade 2 listed building with a pale blue arch and with a white angel like figure looking benevolently over the grounds like a beacon of welcoming arms, nevertheless, the place held the darkest of secrets, in many instances the worst kind of abuse any impressionable young kid could suffer being horrendous child abuse committed by the allegedly devout Sisters of Nazareth.

When the children's mother and father occasionally visited, they did so begrudgingly, however, Robert and his brother Paul formed a remarkably close relationship, sticking together looking after one another. It has also been said that the four siblings regarded the nuns as 'family' forming a close bond while the parents were regarded as outsiders – and here we must pause, because it will be informative to learn that according to an investigation carried out by the *Independent*, 16 August 1998, former residents of the Catholic Nazareth Order's homes confirmed that they suffered appalling, systematic cruelty.

As some little background, for more than 100 years, the Poor Sisters of Nazareth had cared for children in the Order's dozens of homes across Britain. Orphans, such as the Maudsley's, abandoned babies and children deemed uncontrollable or accused of petty crimes were all placed into the hands of these nuns who, to the outside world, epitomised kindness and compassion. And, in an almost Dickensian environment, a secretive place behind locked doors, the nuns with filthy anti-Christian habits maintained a ruthless regime: beatings and acts of extreme cruelty were commonplace, the 'survivors' say. And together, with the spartan existence in the home, gave the kids' lives of utter misery. So, in this context we can start to see – because we can never truly imagine it all – what a dysfunctional start in life Robert Maudsley had. It could also be said that it were the Poor Sisters of Nazareth and dysfunctional parents that formed the bedrock character that is Robert Maudsley to this very day. As for the nuns responsible for this horrific abuse, the least they might have expected is a damned good thrashing - a lynching more appropriate maybe?

But this is not the end of young Robert Maudsley's problems by a long chalk, for after a few years the four children were returned to their parents and by gosh, hadn't they now been busy bees in the bonking department by adding another eight children to their dysfunctional family as Mr Maudsley said: 'We didn't have a TV!'

Indeed, and it says much for the degree of their ill-treatment back home that brother Paul was to claim, although not tongue-in-cheek, staying in the orphanage was: '…the happiest time of our lives.' Beatings by the father were the norm with a stick, slipper or a boot or whatever took the patriarch's fancy, with Robert taking the brunt of the punishment; his mother simply egging her husband on as if she was sadistically enjoying every moment. So, it will come as no surprise that the lad took to running away from home to sleep rough, then upon returning would get even more harsher thrashings over and over again.

To prevent Robert from running away again, George Maudsley locked him in a bedroom for six months, the door only being opened to provide food and more beatings to be administered to the slowly mentally disintegrating youngster, which is confirmed by his brother Paul, thus cruelly all of this landed Robert back into the arms of 'The Beastly Nuns of Nazareth' once again. A childhood that needed uplifting and unrestrictive free from physical and psychological abuse was ruined. He knew that he needed freedom, so, aged eighteen, he fled to London to seek a better life, or so he thought.

So dear reader, just think about all of that for a moment. I am not suggesting any mitigation for Robert's crimes here, by Christopher Berry-Dee is keen to stress that such child abuse can seriously affect the developing child's mind, its thought processing system, so we can say without any doubt whatsoever, this lad's life was irrevocably 'shit-canned' from the get-go!

It was during the late 60s – 1969 to be precise – that the lure of the lights and riches that London often promises but rarely delivers, Soho in the West End was, and still is, the draw for the wanton seeking adventure, money, and friendships of all the wrong types. Seedy back streets trodden by desperate men seeking sex, drink, drugs, the women dressing up in kinky attire to lure in, excite titillate and rip the mugs off. Yes, the sexy, strip club posters outside these joints portray slim, hot, scantily dressed Hot-to-Trot- Totty, yet the actual 'dancers' are most often like pigs dressed in panties. Doorman, with the intelligence of like apes waiting round doors to drag you in, then when the money disappears you are spat out into the street. Then there are well known hot spots for picking up rent boys ripe for the picking by young and elderly men sordidly seeking the pleasure of young flesh. Indeed, if one was observant, one might see a familiar MP lurking around, or even a High Court judge – His Honour out for a night of 'cottaging', only to sit on his bench the next day to sentence some other sap for exposing his genitals on Clapham Common perhaps with a priest in tow?

A new face on the block, un-violated, unused, Robert Maudsley was a prime target which he became, in turn getting into an expensive drug habit formed out of the need to block out the nightmarish existence he had previously suffered – the day on day abuse he had endured. Drug habits are expensive; an easy living is what is needed so suffering physical pain – to which he was used to – for some can be easy money. Entering an arcade filled with tobacco smoke and strewn with discarded cigarette butts was a local pick-up joint for young ripe and willing game. Sleeping rough and couch surfing, being used and abused along with booze and drugs took its toll on him. Yet, despite this he managed to gain part time employment throughout the West End – washing dishes, becoming an odd job man doing errands to feed his drug habit for he was desperate to fund each fix.

Can the reader imagine just for one minute what this young man had gone through from cradle until right now? Can one envisage having such parents like young Maudsley had? Can one imagine being dumped into a so-called Catholic refuge to be treated in such a cruel and dehumanizing way?

Struggling with mental health again Robert attempted suicide and it was noted by the health system that he said: 'Voices are telling me that I should have killed my mum and dad while I had the chance.' Was this a cry for help or were the suicide attempts efforts to block out the pain from continued use as a rent boy. Were the drugs slowly eating away his personality? Nonetheless, psychiatric hospitals became a regular place of refuge in and out of the local system.

On Wednesday, 13 March 1974, Robert Maudsley awoke with the intention to hurt someone. Having had enough of the daily abuse it was time for him to turn the tables. Leaving his rented room, taking a knife in a sheath with him secreted in one of his pockets, he took a walk to Coventry Street in the London's West End. It connects Piccadilly to Leicester Square. Here he entered the Texas Pancake House, where he met a builder called 'John'. What follows comes from Maudsley's own police statement, as follows:

'I took a knife in a sheath with me I went to the Texas Pancake House, Coventry Street but I could not find someone, so I went to the Playground Arcade, the home for homosexuals. I walked about but again could find no one to hurt. I then found a couple of friends, one of them called John, I do not know his other name he wanted me to go home with him he is the one I killed.'

On the two men meeting up, a short walk to Piccadilly, and a local pub called the White Bear public house at 30 Lisle Street, Soho, a swift drink was had by both. Upon leaving they took a tube north bound on the Piccadilly line to Wood Green, where alighting, Maudsley says:

'…we walked from the station to the house the street I don't know the number it was 65, John told me to wait outside.'

From what Maudsley tell us, and it is believed to be truthful, he waited outside for about five minutes until 'John the Builder' had checked that his landlord wasn't hanging around when he invited Maudsley in for a cup of tea. 'John told me to talk quietly as the landlord was watching telly in the next room', Maudsley told detectives after his arrest. A cup of tea was offered and Robert was given some gay porn magazines. Then, it transpires that 'John the Builder' popped out of the room leaving Robert to enjoy a few damp pages of hard-cum-soft porn, with not a copy of the Holy Bible in sight.

It was at this point – s'cuse the pun – that Robert took a knife out of his pocket, and it all went like this claimed Maudsley:

> We started to kiss and masturbate each other, and I thought of killing him but went on masturbating him thinking the feeling might go away and that I might not feel like killing him in the morning. After we finished kissing and masturbating, we both tried to sleep but we were both restless and started to whisper to each other. We then went to sleep but I still had the feeling I wanted to hurt him.

The following morning, around 8.10am, and claiming he still had the same feeling towards John, Maudsley later told police:

> 'He asked me if I wanted to see some photographs, I replied "yes". All of a sudden, I took the knife in my right hand and rushed across the room and stabbed him in the chest, he fell back on the bed shouting "I've got to get out the blood spurted out'. His head was down by the base of the door I stabbed him in the

back a few times…. I wanted to kill someone nothing else, I could have robbed the house. I put the knife back in the sheath and went upstairs to the bathroom to wash myself… all I remember is John's face and saying, "I'm sorry".'

Fleeing the scene, Maudsley made his way to the clergy house of St. Paul the Apostle Roman Catholic Church at 22 Bradley Road. Here, a woman answered the door. 'I rang the bell and a woman answered. I asked if I could see the vicar [priest] and she told me he was at Holy Communion'. In Maudsley's statement he further said: 'I've killed someone, and she asked me to come back later.' He ran across the road then rang the police from a phone box; telling them he had murdered someone but could not think of the address only the house number '65'. Several attempts were made to relay what he had done but no one seemed to take a blind bit of notice.

Hopping onto the tube back to his flat near Piccadilly Circus, Maudsley changed his blood-covered suit. Further on in the police statement he mentions he had a coffee and hid the knife in the settee. 'I wanted to kill someone else and had to leave. I drank my coffee and left', he said – he was going to his place of work to collect his wages and P45 certificate.

By now, Robert Maudsley was at the end of his tether, 'I couldn't take anymore', he said in his statement, 'I went to a phone box in Piccadilly and called Wood Green nick again, asking: '…have you found the body yet?"' Then he returned to Wood Green to once again phone the police, who finally collected him before he showed the officers the way to No, 65 (no road or street name available). Arriving at the house the police arrested Maudsley and asked him: 'Is there anything you want to say sir?' 'I want to say is this real', replied the suspect with the officer responding with: '…unfortunately young man, this *is* for real!'

After a mental assessment it was determined that Maudsley was unfit to stand trial. He was found a bed at Broadmoor Hospital, sadly, however, no one had a clue what was to come for a real-life Dr Hannibal Lecter type was now residing behind the asylum's grim walls.

And it is here at Broadmoor where things went completely tit's-up, for another highly dangerous patient, called David Cheeseman was first sent there in 1963 for wounding with intent. He had been in and out of 'the system' since 1974 when he was convicted, along with a fellow patient called Roy Speake of the attempted murder of a nurse at Rampton Hospital by hitting the nurse over the head with an iron bar. Found a bed at Broadmoor, and under a 20-year restriction order, Cheeseman and Maudsley now found themselves on the same ward and they struck up a friendship.

On 26 February 1977 (The Queen's Silver Jubilee Year) the two men targeted a paedophile called David Allen Francis. And this was no spontaneous attack by any means. According to Maudsley it was planned when all three were allowed out of their separate locked single rooms and Cheeseman asked for a football to play in the exercise area. Maudsley and Francis kicked the ball about while Cheeseman kept watch from the side, then after the game it was claimed that Chessman asked a nurse to open the boot room to return the ball.

A lethal trap was about to snap shut!

All three men entered the boot room; the door was slammed shut leaving the nurse outside while Cheeseman barricaded the door with two footlockers. Cheeseman and Maudsley put the bootlaces in (some accounts say flex from a record player) and tied Francis up: hands behind his back with his screams being heard throughout the hospital. The alarm was set off – other patients sent back to their rooms and locked up for their safety as well as the safety of the staff, and what followed makes for shocking reading.

Maudsley and Cheeseman began a nine-hour torture session, beating Francis who was screaming like a banshee as described by former staff. Through the toughened plastic peephole they could get a glimpse of what was unfolding, unable to help and for Francis things were going to get a lot worse. Unknown to the staff, Maudsley was fashioning a pointed tool out of a spoon smuggled in earlier and he begun to stab at Francis now screaming in agony and pleading for them to stop; raining down punches and kicks at their terrified the shit out hostage with staff still looking through the scratched plastic peephole helpless to do anything at all. Staff allegedly reported Francis's screams were becoming more desperate, pitiful, and quite naturally causing distress to those outside who could only listen and hope that some mercy would be shown. The hours got longer, and the screaming got louder, and it was only after nearly nine hours had passed when a deathly silence fell. Viewed through the scratched plastic it could be seen that Francis's head had been topped like a boiled egg and an implement that used to be a spoon popped into the open skull. The incident had come to a deathly conclusion. When the door was forced open by staff, some reported seeing sperm like matter spread over the room and over Francis's pitiful body. It was claimed that Maudsley had eaten part of Francis's brain earning him the moniker of 'Hannibal the Cannibal'.

It was later said that this tasteless brain eating issue was open to debate. In Geoffrey Wansell's book, *Pure Evil: Inside the Minds and Crimes of Britain's Worst Criminals,* he writes: '…they held his [Francis's] head aloft so that the staff could see his body through the spyhole.' Another account came from a former prison officer. In a July 2018 piece in the Liverpool *Echo*, the officer says that: '...in reality, Maudsley did not eat any part of his victim's brains. In fact, he made a makeshift weapon by splitting a plastic spoon in half to create a rough pointed weapon. He then killed his fellow Broadmoor patient by ramming it into his victim's ear, penetrating the brain,' adding: 'Inevitably, the plastic spoon blade was covered in gore, which was alleged to be his brains.' However, this is contradicted elsewhere when it is said that Francis was garroted to death.

And it is at this point that matters get even more topsy-turvy, for even though we find the allegedly mentally unbalanced Maudsley under lock and key in a mental hospital because he was judged unfit to stand his trial for the previous murder of 'John the Builder', this time around he was found to be mentally competent enough to be convicted of manslaughter – shifted as fast a prison van could move him and dumped in HMP Wakefield which has been dubbed by the media 'Murder Mansion'.

But what of Mr Cheeseman…well after what appears to have been another botch-up, after turning to God, he was subsequently freed from HMP Hollesley Bay open prison in Woodbridge, Suffolk, changed his name to 'Lant', married a French woman from Norfolk, was arrested and cleared of attempted rape a 16-year-old Suffolk girl in a Thurston caravan park and no less than five other sexually related offences while on day-release from prison. In July 2006, at Ipswich Crown Court, the then 65-year-old was acquitted of all charges, nevertheless, for once and to their credit, the Parole Board believed that the sex '…was not consensual…' which flew in the face of the acquittal, and that Lant aka Cheeseman must stay in prison for the remainder of his life. Then get this… of course this God-awful murdering piece of scum challenged the Parole Board's decision and 'demanded' at the taxpayers' expense a fresh hearing, taking his case to the High Court in London. His barrister, Stanley Best did his best, arguing that the fact the hearing was conducted in such a way his 'client' could not see his 'alleged victim was unfair.' Box of tissues, please. However, adding to Lant's sniveling gripes was that as well as '…not being able to see his victim, the way the room was positioned meant that he could not hear everything thing she said.' Oh, bless him!

Notwithstanding, the appeal failed with Judge Michael Kay QC saying that the appeal was 'totally without merit,' adding: 'She [the young girl] was, for the second time, having to give evidence about highly distressing sexual activity in relation to Mr Lant.'

Well, done Judge Kay, well done you!

But what defies belief is the fact that this evil Cheeseman/Lant sex monster/killer with his appalling record of brutality, was ever allowed to walk the streets of Suffolk on day release from prison and enjoy the privilege of allowing him to work at a Salvation Army hostel in Ipswich? Has the world gone completely bonkers…well the then local MP, David Gummer, certainly flipped his own lid when he learned of this…the local constabulary went ape, with Gummer asking the Home Office: 'There must be serious questions about someone who has such a history, irrespective of the case in which he is not guilty?'

The Home Office, using its usual 'Not Our Fault, Guv' line of BS, replied: 'All prisoners are rigorously risk-assessed before release on temporary licence and no prisoner is released if there are concerns for public safety.' Jesus Christ! 'public safety? Had not an already violent Mr Cheeseman not so long back teamed up with another certified nutcase aka Robert Maudsley, kicked a football around the grounds of one of the most notorious, allegedly secure mental asylums on Planet Earth, to then lock him into a room and torture him death over some nine hours while nonce David Allen Francis screamed the place down as staff peered through a spyhole unable to do anything at all.

Adding to this wishy-washy, pen pushing, paper-shuffling attempt to duck for cover, the Home Office official rambled on with: 'In the vast majority of cases, prisoners treat this opportunity properly in accordance with the position of trust they have been given…Our absolute priority is public protection and rehabilitating offenders is a vital part of that…' blah, blah, blah.'

However, one merely has to look up HMP Hollesley Bay's dismal absconder record…it seems that anyone can more-or-less wander off anytime they so choose. But your author has digressed because it is Maudsley who heads up this chapter and his story is far from finished.

After leaving HMP Parkhurst and upon his arrival at HMP Wakefield, the officers made a serious misjudgement, for having recently murdered a paedophile in Broadmoor and doing very nasty things with a plastic spoon, Maudsley, now only twenty-five-years-old, was placed into the general prison population which contained child killers, paedophiles, sex offenders and murderers, thus, during the morning of Friday, 28 July 1978, somewhat predictably the proverbial hit the spinning fan once again and one Salney Derwood, a convicted wife killer, was soon, himself, to become very dead, and it went like this.

Maudsley invited Derwood into his cell, then, using a 'shank' made from a sharpened toothbrush, he slit his throat and stuffed Derwood body under his bunk. Not satisfied he had achieved his homicidal day's work he then went on the prowl for a second victim. Entering Bill Roberts's cell he smashed the man's head against a wall so hard that the skull opened. With two jobs done and dusted Maudsley then walked calmly into the wing's office, placed the shank on the desk and said to the prison officers: 'You will be two short for roll call tonight!'

Robert Maudsley was convicted of double murder. He is now considered the most dangerous man in British 'correctional system' and for that reason he is held in a cell within a cell in the bowels of Wakefield Prison. A Perspex cell 18 feet by 14 feet, and it is believed without verification that this is where the idea for the cell in the film *The Silence of the Lambs* came from. Cardboard furniture, one hour exercise a day under escort with six warders, only visits from two brothers and one nephew are allowed. In 2000 he pleaded to the authorities to let him take a cyanide pill. A five-day hearing in Liverpool dismissed the notion.

As a final note, for a short while in 1991, Maudsley was incarcerated at HMP Parkhurst on the Isle of Wight, and where the prison psychiatrist, Dr Bob Johnson, struck up a relationship with this stone-cold killer. He has said this:

'I visited the prison in May 1991, and I was taken around the hospital wing, and as we are going around, this is, and they opened the main cell door and then there is a wire mesh door inside that there is this gaunt figure, looking like Moses, long straggly hair, miserable as sin, sunken face…so I made a mental note and thought this is somebody I am going to have to work hard to get alongside…and it took me two or three years to get permission from the senior medical officer to go into the hospital and start sessions with Robert Maudsley.

'Initially for me it was quite tricky because I saw him in his cell, and he was sitting on his bed near the window, and I stand near the door. And I said to him, "If you frighten me, I'm going." So, we started talking about his past and got a bit too close and he said: "My palms are getting sweaty", so I ran to the door to let you know. We had this understanding and at that time he had no interest in me to possibly help him. We got an understanding. We got an understanding and that's the key and we were working well…'

At interview, Dr Johnson asked Maudsley: 'How would you describe the progress that you are making?'

Maudsley: 'The progress of the type, I think you've come into the room with me, even though at a distance. I'm able to talk about things a lot more things today, that was able to say six or nine months ago…you see the thing is Bob, well, I say I know, I know in the past when I've tried to face these things, you know, I…'

Dr Johnson: 'Go on then, try to face these…'

Maudsley: 'I'm just capable of doing anything, Bob. And that's why I have got to be cautious Bob, you know.'

If the reader would like to hear the voice of Robert Maudsley talking to Dr Bob Johnson, he can be heard on a Google sourced video titled: *Chilling Interview* dated 21 November 2019 @ 2:52 minutes.

In conclusion, how can we judge Robert Maudsley and the very 'system' in which he has found himself? What we do know is that following his first homicide he was judged as *not* being mentally fit to stand his trial, and the general yardstick for such determinations is based on the 'M'Naughton Rule' – when there is a defence in a criminal case of insanity: that every man is to be presumed to be sane, and that to establish a defence on the grounds of insanity, it must be clearly proved that, at the time of the committing of the act, the party accused was labouring under such a defect of reason, from disease of the mind, as not to know the nature and quality of the act he was doing: or 'if he did know it, that he did not know he was doing was wrong'.

Of course, Maudsley knew all along that killing his first victim was wrong. He knew that his actions were unlawful. His planning and post-crime behaviour was one of a person who knew this all too well. Did his misuse of drugs; his heavy drinking and his rent boy activities all combined contribute to a 'disease of the mind'? We think not. How convenient it was then for him to be given a bed in Broadmoor…some medication, *some* level of close staff monitoring, only to place him in a ward where compassionate nursing staff allowed him to mix freely with men as almost has dangerous as he?

But was this Broadmoor's fault? Of course, it wasn't. This method of looking after their patients has long been embedded since the hospital's inception, so it would be so easy to point the finger at any individual staff for trying to accommodate and please their charges' recreational needs. Simply put, once behind bars and high walls, Maudsley would have killed another person wherever he was incarcerated – secure hospital or prison proper for his record of extremely violent behaviour is writ large throughout.

No, the fault in this case rests with a criminal justice system – to label anyone such as Maudsley as insane when he is anything but; for he can be articulate. He is very bright and well able to fool anyone with his softly-spoken almost 'gayish' chit chat – with the proviso when it suits him, of course! He is a manipulating criminal psychopath, so let us not forget this either… but psychopathy is *not* a disease of the mind. I stress 'not a disease of the mind'.

We also note that following the dreadful torture killing of David Francis by Maudsley/Cheeseman, Broadmoor judged that even some of their own highly dangerous patients/inmates and staff, were in great risk of these two evil men, so both were shipped out: Maudsley initially to HMP Parkhurst, Cheeseman to finally end up in an open prison where he was set free into society by a Leftie system to commit very serious sexual offences again and again…and as the FBI will confirm, with such offenders homicide will inevitably result if not apprehended or kept behind bars.

It goes without saying that no one within the 'system' is ever held responsible for misjudgment, lax of duty, for this *is* the way the 'system' works. It is *always* a case of 'passing the buck'. No one is fired or sued for negligence or demoted…indeed, the opposite is true for more often than not one is promoted. During the research for this book the authors discovered that those who might, or should have been at least reprimanded, have been promoted or gagged for fear of losing their jobs, their livelihood, their homes. What a shocking indictment this is.

Dr Bob Johnson got it one when he said that Robert Maudsley is perhaps one of the most dangerous people he has ever met. Robert Maudsley is well beyond any form of psychological help as Dr Johnson indicates and he was prudent in staying very close to the door. But here is the rub…it was Maudsley who invited Dr Johnson into his cell, not vice versa. Maybe Dr Johnson had prison guards close by, maybe Maudsley was in restraints - I don't know this – but if Maudsley had erupted Dr Johnson could have been killed in a heartbeat. Period… end of story!

***

Daniel Gonzalez.

'You've got the body + I've got the brains.'

Song by Chris Zabriski, adapted for the second Nightmare on Elm Street
movie, Freddy's Revenge, and Freddy Krueger's famous one-liner

Born a Gemini on Saturday, 21 June 1980, Daniel Gonzales was, one can say, raised on the right side of the tracks. Living in pleasant Southwood Avenue, Knaphill, Surrey; his English-born mother Lesley Savage, separated in 1986 from his Spanish father, whom she merely described as a 'domestic partner', so, we cannot say there was ever to become any *Nightmare on Southwood Avenue*, but we would be wrong for all would become *very* wrong - and very soon thereafter.

By the age of ten, Daniel's mother was becoming extremely concerned about his behaviour. School friends had noticed that he was often overheard talking to himself then bursting into fits of uncontrollable laughter for no apparent reason. On some occasions, he drew offensive cartoons and placed drawing pins on his fellow pupils' chairs. Indeed, the 'talking to oneself' is often manifested in people with schizotypal personality disorders. Generally, they have difficulties forming relationships and experience extreme anxiety in social situations: suffer from confused thinking; prolonged depression; feelings of extreme highs and lows; excessive fears and worries; harbour strong feelings of anger; strange thoughts as in delusions and suicidal thoughts. If we add to this the drawing pins, we find 'picquerism', from the French 'to prick'. This can also take the form of cutting aka self-harming, and perhaps the most famous historical incident of picquerism comes from London's 19th- century serial killer, Jack the Ripper. In 1888, this still yet unidentified monster killed five women and mutilated their bodies, often stabbing or cutting into them. So, in exhibiting this – some might say, mild picquerism behaviour at such an early age shows a sadist also in the making. And, it would be fair to say that Lesley Savage had *every* good reason to be worried about Daniel. She became frantic when the boy was expelled from his secondary school because he had now become a physical threat to not only staff but to the other pupils. It seems that from such a young age Daniel Gonzales was destined to become someone to claim dreadful infamy.

In 1998, Humfrey Jonathon Malins was the Conservative MP for the Woking area. He was, in fact, a travelling MP who sought any seat that the Conservative Party were expected to win. Not much has changed since, has it? In her desperation, Lesley Savage had written to Malins and also to The

Department of Health literally begging for some assistance with her now aged nineteen mentally disintegrating son. She also gave an interview with the *Independent* newspaper and was quoted in saying: 'Every time we asked for help for Daniel, or Daniel did himself, we were told we would wait for a crisis to occur before he could get help needed'.

Asking Malins whether her son: '…must commit murder', it seems that once again her cry for help was, once again, falling on deaf ears. A tormented childhood led him to committing minor thefts from shops. Girls taking a shine to him – some saying he had smoldering good looks for a kid – a Spanish glowing skin some have also said: '…if looks could kill this youngster could.'

Since the age of sixteen Daniel had been into drug taking. To fund his habit he shoplifted, assaulted people and demanded their money, often taking trips to London and getting involved in the rave scene and was regularly seen around East London and the West End. With his drug habit getting worse help was needed and, at the age of 19, he was given a six-month stay at the Oak Tree clinic medium security ward – a local unit within the Priory Hospital, in Woking.

Help, it seems, was now to hand. He was prescribed antipsychotic drugs, was looked after by a psychiatrist, and within this structured environment Gonzales appeared to be doing well, leading staff to believe that Gonzales was 'good to go'. When he was discharged from the clinic he immediately stopped taking the prescribed medication, all of which was to have dire consequences for the future starting with an attempted burglary in the Woking area. Police arrested him, he was charged with assault on police and causing criminal damage. He served six months in prison and was released, only for his condition to worsen – his cries for more help getting more desperate, falling on deaf ears, the upshot being that even his own doctor claiming that Gonzales might be faking mental illness despite receiving this from his patient, Gonzales wrote:

> 'I am not coping well I feel suicidal I need help. I really do need help, now I have tried to cope on my own like a normal human being without help or medication, but I have not managed to succeed. I was admitted to hospital in 1998 under section 37 of the mental health act. I do not want this to happen again, so I really need to go to hospital voluntarily ad receive treatment under the care of the doctors before my mental state gets worse.'
>
> Gonzales: 2003 letter to his doctor.

The reply he received was short. To go to the hospital but nothing was put in place and no further help offered. The system again was failing; yet another person amongst many thousands who was crying for help and a drug habit getting worse.

Gonzalez passed the days by watching horror movies: *Nightmare on Elm Street* and *Friday the 13th* being amongst his favourites, along with video games of the horror genre. On Saturday, 11 September 2004, Gonzalez boarded a train for London then took the Tube to Hackney, East London. He wanted to attend a rave. For our older readers, a 'rave' is an organised dance party at a nightclub, an outdoor festival at a warehouse or other private property, less so held in public spaces typically featuring performances by DJs, a seamless flow of EXTREMLY LOUD dance music all held under flashing lights than can be heard and seen by aliens living in another galaxy. This is probably why some extra-terrestrials visit Planet Earth from time-to-time – probably to complain about the loud fucking noise. Nevertheless, during that evening Gonzalez took a cocktail of drugs; Ecstasy, (MDNA) speed (amphetamines) and Ketamine - the latter normally used to sedate large animals and known drug to dope race horses.

So here we find the already mentally turned upside down Gonzales, at the aforementioned rave and stoned out of his tiny mind. Indeed, this rave, or any other rave come to that, seemed to be Gonzales preferred entertainment at weekends. Furthermore, he was also well-known in East London under the name 'Zippy' after 'Zippy the Pinhead', the fictional character who appears in the American comic strip created by Bill Griffith. 'Zippy' also featured in the TV series *Rainbow*.

Quite when, how and why Gonzales acquired the handle, 'Zippy', we may never know – nor will he either, but he had no long-term relationships with anyone; no long-term girlfriends either, yet, those who sort of knew him said that he was 'cute looking', 'innocent', 'likeable' and 'not shy of any young woman whom took a fancy to him.' Well, they would, wouldn't they when they, too, were probably living in some form of psychedelic hallucinating daze for days on end – you know they types: the ones who think that Angela Merkel is Donald Trump in drag, or that 'The Donald' is the 'Second Coming', when in truth he's merely an obese racist, multiple times bankrupt, a misogynist living under a head of carrot-coloured hair, a man who cannot actually read very much, can't spell either, a draft dodger, tax-dodging pathological liar, yet the Americans elected him to be President of The United States – the most powerful man on Planet Earth. And, at the time of writing, we in the UK ain't fairing much better…step forward Boris Johnson. Another self-serving asshole…similar hair 'style', all of which reminds me of this quote from Nikita Khrushchev: 1990. 'Politicians are the same all over. They promise to build a bridge where there is no river.'

Levity aside, what we do know is that 24-year-old Gonzales managed, by hook or by crook to return to Woking the following day. We don't know precisely how he found his way back to the town, and one might suspect nor did he, but coming down from his high he slept off the cocktail of drugs to wake on Monday 13th.

When I say that he 'slept off the cocktail of drugs', it has to be said that this isn't entirely accurate for, at 8.20am he was running bollock naked through the Knaphill housing estate, passing shops, the Robin Hood public house, children in a school playground ,and scaring to death the grey rinses, some on Zimmer frames too. Not surprisingly, several people called the police saying that a youth is running around Knaphill wielding a todger. With that sort of unique description given of 'The Flashing Zippy', one might have assumed that the Surrey cops would have spotted Gonzales and apprehended him rapido – but one would have assumed wrongly because they didn't! So, where did he go, well here things take an even more bizarre turn, so the reader might wish to sit in a comfortable chair and take a stiff drink!

Lesley Savage had by now found another partner, a likeable chap by the name of Steven Harper, and it was Harper who telephoned Lesley at her place of work to explain that her son had paid an unexpected visit. Lesley came home and entered to find that knives had been thrown all around her kitchen; that he'd smashed a knife down hard on the sink's draining board leaving a mark, that he was naked and sporting a black eye caused by throwing himself face down on the linoleum floor. Indeed, it was later said by Stephen Harper: 'Daniel passed me naked on the driveway…I drove round

Knaphill looking for him. There was [sic] schools open, people about. I couldn't find him…I called the police, but they didn't come.'

But this isn't the end of it by a long chalk. Unknown to his mother, her son was writing letters to himself and these letters to himself were describing to himself – or his other personality or his alter ego – how he would go about murdering people and the satisfaction he would gain from committing such heinous crimes. One letter later found by police went: 'This is the best things I've done in my life'. It was signed 'Zippy'. He had even noted down a 'magic number' it being '10'. This indicated the number of murders he would have to commit before being raised to the rank of 'serial killer'. However, as all of our readers *will* know, one qualifies as a serial murderer once three kills have been committed with cooling of periods between the 'events'. No need 'Zippy' to overdo it my lad. Three would have been enough by a long chalk.

The town of Woking is situated on the train line between London Waterloo terminating at Portsmouth Harbor, to be precise, and Wednesday, 15 September 2004 would become a day that a Portsmouth couple, Peter King, aged 61, and his wife Janice would never forget for they were taking a leisurely stroll in an area known by the locals as Portsbridge Creek in the Hilsea area of the city. Indeed, if you have a mind to look the place up on Google Maps, it's a delightful walk – if it's not raining. And Gonzales was taking a walk in that area at the same time as Peter and Janice.

At about 9am that Wednesday, Gonzales had taken a steak knife from a kitchen drawer, packed some clothes into a rucksack and he took the train from Working to Portsmouth, where he probably alighted at Cosham. Making his way from the station, he walked south along the A397 towards the

Portsbridge roundabout, then along the waterway where he came upon the Kings walking their dog down a narrow path next to derelict gun emplacements. Gonzales yelled at the couple: 'I'm gonna kill you', then Gonzales attacked Peter King, slashing and stabbing him under the chin. Peter put up a tremendous fight to protect himself and his wife which culminated in them ending up in bushes with Gonzales shouting: 'Sorry, I'm schizophrenic…I can't help it,' before running off.

His blood lust unsatisfied with the hue and cry now raised, Gonzalez then boarded a train east-bound for Worthing, West Sussex, with intentions to find another victim. He had one thing in mind – to take a life. Popping into a local shop near the station he stole a knife and a white hockey mask and started trawling the alleyways, to then follow a man who suddenly turned left onto a main road – thus the intended attack was thwarted.

We next find this lone wolf waiting in bushes along a country path off Oakdean Crescent, Highdown, just a short distance from Worthing. This time his target was grandmother/pensioner 73-year-old Marie Harding. Gonzales stabbed the elderly lady in the back and slit her throat before rummaging through her purse for twenty pounds as she bled to death. He then returned to Woking by train, keeping himself busy on the journey by writing up in what he called his 'diary' the account of his first murder.

Scribbling away, he noted down: 'I will be a serial killer. I mean it, I promise. I will be a serial killer. I got that old bitch proper, bloodbath, pouring out of her throat, boy, McFlurry! I got to say this, it felt really, really, really good. One of the best things I've done in my life.'

Gonzalez spent part of Thursday, 16 September at home; leaving in the afternoon to start binge drinking and taking drugs in a local pub before boarding a train bound for London's Waterloo, then to the West End where he shoplifted two large kitchen knives. Now staggering from pub to pub he eventually caught a night bus to Tottenham in north London where he arrived at 4am on the Friday.

Amiable Irish-born former pub landlord, Kevin Molloy, aged 46, was walking home after a drink in the Swan public house in High Road. Of large build and tall, Kevin was known by his pals as a gentle giant; a loveable hail-fellow-well met chap who had no enemies at all. Then, at 5.30am he came across Gonzales who pulled a knife and in a despicable and horrid attack began slashing Molloy in the face, then in the stomach and eventually thrusting the blade into his chest killing Molloy there and then. The body being found an hour later on the pavement.

> 'He [Molloy] was just some bloke walking down the road and I pulled a knife out and stabbed him. As I was stabbing him, he said: "What the hell are you doing?" So, I said to him: "Are you stupid? I'm killing you," and I killed him.'
>
> Gonzales: statement to police

Following the almost demonic blitz killing of Kevin Molloy, Gonzales dumped the two stolen knives in a park then walked the streets for four miles; ringing doorbells and knocking doors until he eventually came across the address of the Constantino family who lived in Frobisher Road, Hornsey, and here, at 7am, he broke in, most probably to find more knives.

Koumis Constantino, aged 59, and his wife Christella, were woken by the sound of breaking glass. For his part, Gonzales had rifled through a kitchen drawer and selected an 8-inch blade. Koumis came upon the intruder in the hallway, so he picked up a child's cradle to defend himself. But this could not prevent this drug-crazed madman from plunging the knife into his arm and chest.

'The cradle fell down and he [Gonzales] tried again to stab me. I grasped him by the hand. He bit me in the right hand, and I bit him on the neck' Koumis later told police. Indeed, it seems that on this occasion 'Zippy' had bitten off more than he could chew for he certainly did not consider that Christella would lay into him with her slipper before rushing out of the house to scream for help. And it was at this point that Gonzales dropped the knife and fled. Covered in blood, fueled on adrenalin and ecstasy, he took a taxi to Highgate where he would commit his most savage attack of all.

Four miles on his way into Highgate, Gonzales told the taxi driver to stop; he paid the fare and wandered off. Whether or not the driver noticed that his fare was literally drenched in blood or not matters little in the scheme of things, but what happened next mattered am awful lot.

75-year-old retired pediatrician Derek Robinson, and his wife Jean, a 60-year-old music teacher, were having breakfast in their home at 24 Makepeace Avenue, Highgate Hill, when their doorbell rang. It was 'Zippy' the monster from Hell, and what happened next is a real-life Stephen King nightmare story coming true, but on this one there are two accounts of what happened – one being that Gonzales broke into the house in search of another knife, and that he found a 6-inch blade in the Robinson's kitchen or, as previously mentioned, he rang the doorbell and things unfolded from there – it's a mixed murder bag, it really is.

Gonzales later revealed: 'As soon as I got in there I actually stood there and had a breather and I thought okay 'Ready steady go' and then I did it,' all of which counters the ringing of the doorbell scenario altogether. Gonzales must have got the blade from the kitchen drawer because he told police: 'I stabbed him [Derek] once and stabbed him again. I wanted to kill him quickly, so I stabbed him in the throat…the woman was really strong. I started feeling really sorry for her. I went through her throat then I just stabbed her loads of times in the heart because I wanted her to die quickly…I felt clean, orgasmic. I had washed all the crap out of my life. I felt better,' he added with a smug smile over his face.

Unfortunately for 'Zippy', minutes after the attack a decorator called at the house to find blood spattered across the freshly walls. Gonzales, who was interrupted as he stripped naked to take a shower to wash the blood off his body, nonchalantly told him: 'Sorry about this mate', before fleeing the scene.

Still covered in blood, Gonzalez was now running and hiding between roads to avoid the sirens that were blaring out as police rushed to the murder house. The four-and-a-half-mile journey on foot led him to Tottenham Court Road tube station where he attempted to purchase a ticket to Waterloo to get back to Woking. However, one of the station staff noticed blood staining on a twenty-pound note and immediately called for assistance *via* the radio system requesting the police. It has been said that a slight scuffle broke out; nevertheless, he was arrested by police who took him into custody and where he admitted murder.

During the police interviews, Gonzalez kept on repeating: 'I am schizophrenic, and voices told me to do it.' Sometimes he broke down under questioning and sobbed: 'It was very bad. I have had a real shit life. I'm a little boy and I didn't feel very well.' Adding: 'I haven't had a job for four years. I haven't had a girlfriend for ages,' all of which led Detective Inspector David Cobb to believe that Gonzales was a bit too clever for his own good, highly manipulative, and attention seeking in the hope of gaining sympathy and did not want to accept responsibility for his actions. 'I just couldn't handle growing up to be a man. I was just sitting around playing PlayStation. I just couldn't handle anymore,' whined 'Zippy'. 'I should go to the electric chair.' And maybe that would have not been such a bad idea at all for there are always two schools of thought about how a vile, murderous killer like Gonzales, should be treated/punished – no three schools actually.

1: if one of his victims had been one of your own beloved next-of-kin you might have been at the front of the queue to pull the switch, to join other bereaved folk all shouting 'Burn, Gonzales, burn!'

2: you might be a Bible-thumping, God-fearing, forgive all sinners, soul. One to flyspeck his entire narrative in search of some mitigation for his evil deeds. A sort of 'Extreme Leftie', which is all well and good until some asswipe shits all over your parade or hacks your grandma to death and lets her bleed out while he nicks a few quid from her purse.

3: but if you are a (3) you will be a 'fence-sitter'; unable to form an opinion one way or another, you will be thinking, 'Yay, Broadmoor'…. Pass the parcel, pass the buck, so let's find a bed for Gonzales there, fill him full of drugs – he likes drugs – and let's throw away the key.'

To await his March 2006 trial, Gonzales was remanded in HMP Belmarsh, but staff here started raising concerns about his state of mental health – exactly the same concerns his mother, Lesley, had been raising concerns about for years. Yes, Broadmoor seemed to be the best opt-out, so he was placed in the Special Care Unit, which was considered to have highest security protocol in the UK.

And it was here that he insisted on terrifying other patients with reenactments of his murders.

One afternoon Gonzalez, not content with showing others what he done, started to chew on his right arm. Once he started, he then made an effort to gnaw on his wrist, allegedly to commit suicide by biting himself to death. It was said that his veins were the target, teeth tearing into his flesh, but fortunately the intervention of staff stopped the incident – the extent of his injuries is unknown, nonetheless, he was treated for his self-inflicted injuries at Frimley Park Hospital.

Although many might disagree, Gonzales's defence team at his Old Bailey trial faced an uphill struggle from the outset; their task not helped one bit because their client was as guilty as sin. Indeed, their only goal was to argue a case that would convince the court to find Gonzales to be insane under the McNaughton Rule, or at best something along the lines of 'diminished mental capacity', thus not totally responsible for the offences charged.

Acting upon instructions from their client, the defence claimed that Gonzales was subject to 'hearing voices' and that he was a schizophrenic. That he compared his murder spree to that of the horror films *Halloween* although which particular one out of the series they failed to pin down: was it the 1978 flick, *Halloween II* (1981), or *Halloween III* (1982)?

Defence also mitigated that their client also wanted to know how Freddy Krueger from the slasher movie *Nightmare on Elm Street*, felt like for the day. Indeed, Gonzales denied murder claiming that voices were the ones who told me to kill people it was not him – at once signally failing to explain whose voices he'd actually heard.

The court heard that Gonzalez had told doctors that he was bored, and that is what drove him to rampage kill. Consultant shrink, Dr Edward Petch, who had examined Gonzalez, said: 'I have never seen anything like this…the degree of disturbance was without parallel in my experience.' He may have been correct, for during the trial Gonzales had requested a holding cell visit: he wanted to talk to his mother and stepfather, but he attacked them with guards and police having to intervene. Nevertheless, the jury took just sixty-minutes to find Gonzales guilty of murder and the stony-faced judge gave out six life sentences without any chance of release, but of course Gonzales was allowed to appeal this life term, with his lawyers arguing that life was too long a tariff and asking that the sentence be reduced to thirty years. However, justice prevailed. Due to the prisoner's age and the state of his mind, life would mean exactly that. He would die behind bars, only to be released wearing a pine box, however, Gonzales's stay at Broadmoor was relatively short but not sweet for it would not only become eventful for him but the staff too. He would challenge the staff at every opportunity and was considered to be the most unpredictably violent patient in the place.

For example, one afternoon a six-man 'Open & Close Team' was called to move him. Putting up a determined fight for a man with a small build, consultants were now extremely concerned that he was almost out of hand.

At this point in the book the author stresses that there is a rigid dichotomy between the treatment of mentally disturbed people in secure hospitals and hardened criminal incarcerated in 'proper' prisons. In Broadmoor the majority of patients having been given a bed there behave themselves once they have become adjusted to their new life's regime. Of course, some may 'kick off' from time-to-time, but in the main the staff are there to 'care' for their charges, not punish them. Nevertheless, Broadmoor has set procedures and CCTV covers every angle with, quite obviously, radio communication being used throughout the hospital. Patients when moved about are noted, so 'A' does not meet 'B' if they are considered a danger to each other. This is a preventative measure to reduce conflict between patients, because as we have already noted, they have been known to kill each other or attack someone unprovoked. During an incident in the 90s the exterior siren system was activated not for an escape, only for patients going on the rampage. We must also remember the volatility that exists within the walls of the hospital, and it takes a split second for some of the more dangerous patients a chance to pounce. A slight glare of the eye, a whisper of abuse from patient to patient and all hell may break loose.

A day in the hospital is like any other day… nothing changes, same routines, same faces and the same hospital food. Even for patients the request for a drink is taken to a new level. High riskers are kept locked in their rooms and two members of staff are needed one to open the door the other to place the drink down with the patient told to move to the back of the room. A quick move back and the door is closed and locked, it's for everyone's safety, so invariably no chances are taken.

So, this was the daily routine for Gonzalez, who along with trying to impress other patients with his past acting out of the murders and attacks he had committed, one might have thought think that the hospital would have learned that Gonzalez was getting slowly worse. Psychiatric one-to-one counseling and the administration of drugs were having no effect. During August a jeweled CD case was smuggled into his room and, upon opening his door on the morning of 9 August 2007, staff came across the lifeless body of Gonzalez. The CD case had been broken and his blood was oozing onto the floor from the cuts to his wrists and arms. Almost, it seems, under the eyes of staff an extremely high-risk patient had yet again committed suicide. The 'Blame Game' was to start again.

Reports in 2007 listed faults with the NHS; one recording that Gonzalez had had some sixty mental health appointments and that Surrey police had lost notes that referred to earlier incidents. The Independent Office for Police Conduct found that the force was not at fault for not listening to Gonzalez's mother and not at fault for the incident on 13 September 2004 where they were unable to locate him running around Knaphill in his birthday suit. Gonzales's mother Lesley Savage and her partner Steven Harper say police could have averted the two-day killing spree if they had acted on their requests for help and had had him detained under the Mental Health Act. Your author suggests that there can be no doubt that had the police, in full knowledge of this man's violent and mentally disturbed behaviour, acted swiftly then the following murders would not have occurred. But herein lies the rub, for a statement taken from the receptionist at Woking police station is at odds with Mr Harper's statement and was 'conveniently' lost along with other paperwork, with police saying they knew nothing of Gonzales's naked rampage and that Harper made no complaint at all – at least it seems to be that way. No way would the police take the rap so the buck would have to fall someplace else, but as in all of these types of cases the buck stops nowhere and never will.

We might also say: 'so what indeed because the police were off the hook in any event, and we can't turn the clock back can we? Can we apportion any blame on Broadmoor staff –maybe not. We recall the dichotomy referred to earlier, for although being a secure mental hospital, Broadmoor is, in effect, a prison too. So, it seems that wherever Gonzales was confined, his behaviour was so extreme, so pathologically antisocial, he was so prone to terrible outburst of violence – even homicidal violence – so completely evil, that no place on Planet Earth could have changed that. No drugs or counseling could have altered anything either, all of which brings us to ask the question: was Gonzales insane as in mad?

Legally, Gonzales was not insane. He was certainly fit enough and mentally competent enough to understand that when he was committing his crimes that what he was doing was wrong, and being fit to stand his trial for murder and instructing his lawyers was echoed in his total grasp of the proceedings at the Old Bailey. In fact, the author agrees with Detective Inspector David Cobb who quickly came to the opinion that Gonzales was a self-serving manipulative, whining psychopath: an attention seeker; moreover, self-mutilation is a way that these types of people try to gain sympathy from others, in much the say as those who threaten to commit suicide but never get round to leaping off the Clifton Suspension Bridge or over the cliff at Beachy Head. Harsh words, indeed, so let's not get to into this 'Nanny State' mentality. Some people are born to become evil, and fortunately for us they are few and far between.

And, so what if Daniel Gonzales was into movies such as *Friday the 13th*, or *Nightmare on Elm Street*, or that he watched 'Zippy' on the box? So, what if he did waste away much of his time glued to violent video games while stoned out of his tiny mind on booze and drugs? It could be said that while initially the authorities dismally failed to heed his mother's desperate cries for help, at the end of the day there can be absolutely no mitigation for her son's actions for all of the blame must fall upon him.

Yes, this evil monster Gonzales took his own life, and it was probably the most decent thing he had ever done and the UK is a far better place for it. Harsh words, indeed!

***

Ronald 'Ronnie' Kray.

'Hey, you. Get this gentleman a Coke and be quick about it!'
Ronnie Kray to a Broadmoor staff member when being interviewed by author
Christopher Berry-Dee.

'Who loves you, eh? That's right, Mummy loves you, you little monsters. Mummy loves you.'

Violet Kray to Ronnie and Reggie aged 3.

For decades now, Reggie and Ronnie Kray have become synonymous with Gangland London, and what has not been researched and written about this violent duo one could put on a postage stamp, however, this chapter is not about their lives of crime, it is about what deteriorating mental condition brought Ronnie to Broadmoor Hospital. It is not a pleasant story. Many look back at the Krays with some form of reverence, but in the grand scheme of criminal underworld things, and even when compared with the gangs and mobsters of today, they are not 'big time' at all. Indeed, when we compare them with the John Gottis of this world, they were small fry.

With that said and to back up a bit, the two boys were born ten minutes apart late on 24 October 1933, in a small, terraced house at number 68 Stean Street, Hoxton, Borough of Hackney, London. Indeed, Hoxton was so far down the social scale it was even frowned upon by people from other deprived parts of East London. Traditionally, the only ways of escaping its poverty were either through boxing or crime – often both.

The patriarch, 26-year-old Charles David 'Charlie' Kray Sr, was a wardrobe dealer who persuaded people to sell him clothes, silver and gold for resale at a profit. He was a gambler; a spendthrift who had little influence on the twins' upbringing. He was a deserter during World War II, and on the run from the police for twelve years and was, therefore, rarely at home.

The matriarch was 23-year-old Violet. The couple already had a six-year-old son, also called Charlie, who was born in 1926. A daughter, Violet, born in 1920, died in infancy; the family's heritage was a combination of Irish, Jewish and Romany descent – a genetic cocktail indeed.

Ronnie's childhood started with an early illness, Diphtheria, as did Reggie who made a swift recovery, but Ronnie was held in hospital and the family was not allowed to visit. Diphtheria is a very serious, possibly fatal infection, caused by strains of bacteria called 'Corynebacterium diphtheriae' that makes a toxin (poison) causing people to get very sick. It is usually spread from person to person through respiratory droplets, like from coughing and sneezing. People can also fall ill from touching infected open sores or ulcers. However, Violet was having none of this hospitalization of Ronnie and despite the highly contagious nature of her boy's condition she stormed into the place, picked up Ronnie and walked out with him screaming: 'I AM HIS MOTHER!', despite much protest from the nurses.

It has been posited (without any evidence to prove it) that Diphtheria was the cause of Ronnie's later mental issues, but this would have been highly unlikely, so perhaps a little later on we might look elsewhere. Needless to say, that throughout the boys' childhood, Violent was the dominant figure in the twins' lives. She doted on them, always taking care to treat them with scrupulous equality. She herself had come from a very strict family upbringing. Violet's teetotal father, John Lee, always insisted that his three daughters had to be in by 9pm every evening. And, so, when she was just 17, she eloped to marry Charlie Kray, whereupon her father disowned her.

After giving birth to Charlie, the twins' elder brother, Violet started to see her own parents occasionally. But it was only after the arrival of the twins, who rapidly established themselves as his favourite grandchildren that she was allowed to visit her father's house on a regular basis. The boys first attended Wood Close School and the Daneford Street School and, in 1939, the family moved to 178 Vallance Road, Bethnal Green. The small Victorian two-up, two-down terrace house became known as 'Fort Vallance'.

'Number 178 was a lucky old house. It had a big oak door with a large knocker, and people used to call it 'Fort Vallance'. It was a terraced house with a toilet out in the yard. Ron and I used to love the kitchen. We had a big coal fire and we used to sit around it while our mother used to be doing the ironing or making pots of stew or cups of tea.'

Reggie Kray: in his autobiography *Born Fighter* 1991.

And as was the previous address, this part of Bethnal Green was no Knightsbridge either – case in point being that the area surrounding the house was known as 'Deserter's Corner' due to the large number of men living in the street who had deserted the army or had ignored their call-up papers. Aside from the toilet, in the Kray's backyard was a chicken pen and later a grinder for Ronnie's collection of bayonets and swords. From the moment the twins moved in they both shared a room at the back of the house and continued to live there on and off until they were imprisoned.

Reggie was slightly brighter and more outgoing than his twin brother. Even at an early age, he found it easier than Ronnie to talk to people. Ronnie found ways to compensate – either by sulking or screaming to gain attention or trying to outwit Reggie in overblown displays of love for their mother. And it is here we might start to see the seedling of Ronnie's disintegrating pathology. Psychoanalyst, Heinz Kohut (1913-1981) contended that tantrums – especially in children – are narcissistic rages caused by the thwarting of the youngster's grandiose-exhibitionist core. The blow to the inflated self-image when a child's wishes are (however justifiably) refused, creates a fury because it strikes at the feeling of omnipotence. We could, therefore, suggest that Ronnie Kray knew almost from the outset that he was the weaker sibling of the two, however, according to their teachers, the twins were: '…salt of the earth, and never the slightest trouble to anyone who knew how to handle them. If there were anything to be done at school they'd be utterly cooperative…they'd always be the first to help. Nothing was too much trouble.'

Furthermore, each twin would play close attention to every move the other made. Fiercely loyal to each other, they were also the greatest of rivals. If one started a fight the other had to join in. And it was to 'The Noble Art' that both would eventually turn. The influence of their grandfather, John 'Southpaw Cannonball' Lee, led both lads into amateur boxing, which was at that time a popular working class pastime for many East End boys. By 1946, they were feared competitors and are said never to have lost a bout before turning professional at age 28.

To monetarily digress, regaling the twins with his tales of bare-knuckle fighting in Hackney's Victoria Park, 'Grandad Lee' was one of the great east London characters of the inter-war years. He fought as a featherweight and had one of the hardest left-handed punches in his class. He also possessed a huge repertoire of showman tricks, which included licking a white-hot poker and walking along a line of bottles balanced upside down on their tops. Even as an old man, he kept himself fit, punching a discarded mattress hung up in his backyard and, on one occasion, cycling 42 miles to Southend for a family party at the age of 75. He died aged 98 and to Ronnie he was simply: '…the most amazing man I've ever met.'

But the twins' big problem was an inability to confine their violence to the ring. Amid the devastation of the Blitz, on the bombsites and in burned-out buildings they fought rival gangs or boys and quickly earned a reputation as the toughest of scrappers. Rapidly they were learning the art of survival, which included outwitting the forces of law and order and making most of their passion for fighting.

So, all of the social, physical and psychological ingredients had been put in place for the Kray twins to become hardened criminals from the day they were born. They came from an impoverished background; they had a semi-absentee father and a doting mother who came herself from a strict household. Her twins became effectively the sons of bare-knuckle fighter John Lee had always wanted, yet denied him by the gift of three daughters. However, there was one big problem – Ronnie Kray was gay and at that time homosexuality was against the law; homosexuals were frowned upon and they bore the social stigma of being called 'poofs' or 'queers' or 'closet queens', as disgusting as this is to us today.

As much as your author would enjoy regaling you with pages and pages of detail outlining the criminal careers of Ronnie and Reggie Kray, which as we have stated earlier, in the grand theme of today's Gangland World, does not add up to a hill of beans, that they were boxers is all good stuff, but let's face facts for they were lightweights when compared with the American and Russian mafia capos. The Triads would have eaten them for breakfast. 'The Essex Boys', 'The Adams Family', 'The Wembley Mob', 'The Yardies'; Thomas 'Tam' McGraw' and the Scottish gangs, as would have the Brothers Gunn out of Bestwood, Nottingham. Yet, many of us seem to regard the Krays as Robin Hoods who, in reality, didn't exist at all. Nonetheless, it was top cop Leonard "Nipper" Read who was tasked with bringing the twins empire crumbling down.

'Both of us, given the choice, would have preferred to hang.'

Ronnie Kray.

On 8 May 1968 both twins were arrested. At trial held at the Old Baily in front of Judge Mr. Justice Melford Stevenson, both were found guilty of murder and sentenced to the longest sentence handed down out at the time – thirty years each.

'I am not going to waste words on you. In my view society has earned a rest from tour activities.'

Mr Justice Melford Stevenson.

It was also noted as the longest and most expensive trial in British history with Ronnie and Reggie being sent on their own way within the prison system; HMP Durham being one of them and it was also noted that since the age of twenty-two Ronnie suffered from a schizophrenic illness. So, what is 'schizophrenia'?

The broad definition is: '…a severe long term mental disorder of a type involving a breakdown in the relation between thought, emotion, and behaviour, leading to faulty perception, inappropriate actions and feelings, withdrawal from reality and personal relationships into fantasy and delusion, and a sense of mental fragmentation'. Phew, that is a bit long-winded, is it not? So, in fear of being tactless, let's say that a sufferer lives in a world where elephants fly, lead balls bounce and fairies reign supreme, and *our* Ronnie certainly did – did he not? Nevertheless the actual cause of schizophrenia is unknown and currently there is no cure. The good news is that schizophrenia can be 'successfully treated and managed' – the key is to have a strong support system in place and receive the right treatment.

During the 1968 trial, case papers were prepared by Dr Denis Leigh of the Royal Bethlem and Maudsley Hospitals during a five-hour interview to see if the twins were fit to stand trial. Dr Leigh had written that Ronnie claimed he had been '…a very bad scholar, although he could read and write', and he had been: 'slung out' of the Royal Fusiliers aged 18 for assault on a guard.' Dr Leigh recorded Ronnie's marital status: '…as single, no girlfriend and he denies that he is a homosexual'. As Dr Leigh's notes go on, '…Ronnie describes himself as liking classical music, singers and reading biographies with Genghis Khan and Lawrence of Arabia being his favourites,' adding, 'Ronnie is a friendly man not bad tempered'. Somewhat strangely in the notes, Dr Leigh was shown photos of a donkey called 'Figaro', which the family had once kept. When Ronnie was asked by Dr Leigh which specific autobiographies *he had* read on Genghis Kahn and Lawrence of Arabia, our Ron could only recall that Genghis Khan had died while riding a motorbike and Lawrence of Arabia chased Arabs on his elephant. When pressed on what classical music he liked, Ronnie replied: 'Umm, I dunno. But *Down at The Old Bull and Bush* is a good un.'

So, it is at this place in this chapter we should lighten things up a bit, so come on guys and gals, let's get into the spirit of things. Look up Google for the video: *Florrie Forde – Down at The Old Bull and Bush*. It's sing-along time with one of our Ron's favourite pieces of classical music. I love it – well I would, wouldn't I because I am a Cockney born and bred.

In July 1979, Ronnie was shipped off to Broadmoor Hospital - the correct term being that he was 'found a bed there' – so one might think that interest in this villain would die down, but not in our Ronnie. Sacks full of letters, fan mail, various letters from celebrities and visits from the rich and famous kept him occupied. One of the visitor's blonde hair, green eyes, cheekbones sharp enough to shave a man's face along with a voice that millions have listened too, was Debbie Harry from the group 'Blondie'. Actor Richard Burton had visited Ronnie in prison: it was said to get a feeling of a real villain in preparation for the 1971 film aptly named *The Villain*, oddly enough part-filmed in Bracknell just a stone's throw from Ronnie's last place of internment. Barbera Windsor was often a visitor, so was Reggie and Charlie Kray. Christopher Berry-Dee, gives us a first-hand account of his visit: Used with Chris's permission:

'I met Ronnie along with my late friend, oil painter Paul
Lake. In many ways this was a memorable occasion for me
for here I was being greeted warmly by the notorious
Ronnie Kray. Tall, a little stooped he wore an immaculate
dark suit, white shirt cuffs showing, gold cufflinks with
'RK', highly polished shoes. He looked fresh. Fit as a
fiddle, his eyes lively. No sense of being him being sinister
at all.

'We sat down at a table in the spacious visitors'
room. Ronnie asked us what we would like to drink…Diet
Coke…so he snapped his fingers to a guard or some other
hospital employee: "Hey, you," he said, "Get these two
gentlemen a drink. And be quick about it." "Yes, Ron",
came an immediate reply.

'The proverb, 'Time and tide wait for no man',
wrote Geoffrey Chaucer, so my recollections of my hour-
long chat with 'Mr. Kray' are mostly gone now. No signs
of him having any mental illness whatsoever…but then of
course he was heavily medicated. In all of my many years
interviewing many of the world's most highly dangerous
criminal psychopaths, Ronnie came across as a 'Mr Nice
Guy'…but he wasn't, was he?'

Without any doubt, Ronald Kray was schizophrenic and there is some
evidence to suggest that he suffered from Asperger syndrome – the latter not
proven but a few of the signs of affliction were there. We know that just like
his schooling he was a 'good pupil', ever so anxious to please his tutors,

likewise – give or take a few scrapes – he was a model patient while at Broadmoor. It seems that a structured environment suited to bring out the 'best' in Ronnie Kray. So, with this in mind, author Christopher Berry-Dee recalls the words of an old friend, the late Lord Chief Justice of England, the Lord Lane, who wrote while collaborating on Berry-Dee's book *Ladykiller*:

> 'The prospect of a young man spending the rest of his life in prison is appalling. It is a pity that there seems to be no alternative. There is good in the worst of us. Oddly enough, incarceration sometimes serves to allow that fact to be proved.'
>
> Source: *Ladykiller: Did This Man Kill Suzy Lamplugh.* Christopher Berry-Dee and Robin Odell (1992) later re-wrapped as *Prime Suspect: The True Story of John Cannan, The Only Man Police Want to Investigate for The Murder of Suzy Lamplugh* (2008).

Many reasons have been put forward to explain why the Kray twins became violent criminals – the environment they were raised in, the long absences of their father, their rivalry, and so on, but there could have been another factor.

A German study of the 1920s made the startling discovery that if one identical twin had a criminal record, there was a more that 75 percent likelihood that the other twin would have one too. Still more surprising was that fact that this held true whether the twins lived together or not – in some instances, brothers separated for years had remarkably similar criminal narratives. Therefore, the implications of such findings are significant. They suggest that the criminality of the Krays could *possibly* have had more to do with genetic programming than the poverty and villainy of the East End, or the manner in which they were raised.

Live in 'Cloud Cuckoo Land' did our Ronnie Kray most certainly, for one of his obsessions was with the Mafia, especially by the 1920s gangsters like Al Capone. He was intrigued by the possibility of forming an alliance with them and helping them to establish a foothold in London. However, his visit to America to make contact with the Mafia was more like a childhood fantasy than the business trip it was intended to be. He returned to London with very little achieved. As one Mafia 'made man' recalls:

> 'This Ron guy came here all smart and dressed. The moment he opened his mouth we asked: 'London, what the fuck is that a city or a loser's washroom? Legit clubs, give us a break. We move into a place we buy the docks, not some club. What a jerk off.'

So now is the time to say goodbye to Ronnie Kray. We can do this in the nicest way with that old song by Flanagan and Allen, *Underneath the Arches* because Ron would like that, bless his soul.

Ronnie is buried in Chingford Mount Cemetery, London Borough of Waltham Forest, plot BO9. So, if you are passing by, please place a buncha flowers by his headstone. He would like that, too.

***

James Lang.

'What do you think you are, for Chrissake, crazy or
somethin'? Well you're not! No you're not! You're no crazier
than the average asshole out walkin' the streets and that's it.'

Ken Kesey: *One Flew Over the Cuckoo's Nest*.

Was the plan to escape together? Two dangerous Broadmoor patients within weeks of each other, two different crimes but both had something in common: freedom.

The year is 1970 and one of the most despicable heinous crimes had been committed in Hindley, an area in Wigan an area of Greater Manchester. A body of a 12-year-old girl had been found by locals. Susan Young had been missing from home for a few hours. 7 September she had popped out to buy an ice cream from the local shop. Her father raised the alarm when the family realised she was missing and with the help of Lang and neighbours they started to look for her. Unknown to Susan's father Lang had already murdered Susan, hiding her lifeless body under the floorboards of his sitting room. As fate would have it, Lang was the Youngs' next door neighbour, there was nothing suspicious about him at all. This despicable act of trying to help someone find a loved one knowing what they have done is comparable to the likes of child killers Russell Bishop and Ian Huntley, who even appeared on television being interviewed while showing no remorse. The fact that Lang even felt that this action was acceptable is absolutely abhorrent and shows he had no feelings for what he'd to the girl or her family. The long hours of searching produced no results, police now involved along with more neighbours. During the evening Lang got hold of an old-fashioned pram so began the task of taking the floorboards up in the sitting room took up Susan's body and put her in the pram. Leaving the house Young took a short journey of 75 yards to the local Leyland Park. It was said this action took place between late Saturday evening and early Sunday morning; Lang then dumped the child's body in a ditch. Fingers pointed to Lang fairly quickly. Unknown to locals Lang had been released from prison after serving three years for rape. This only surfaced after the court case in which Lang was convicted of manslaughter with the court believing his lawyer's plea - the old chestnut of diminished responsibility. Psychiatrists' reports were submitted giving Lang a free pass to Broadmoor in 1971. Previous convictions show sexual assaults, theft, and rape. Previously serving prison terms for a variety of offence, now he's conveniently given a bed in Broadmoor.

'Nonce' is the acronym for 'Not On Normal Communal Exercise', and it was once used by warders as a note fixed to patient's doors so not to mix child molesters with others inside Broadmoor, and yes it was first used inside the asylum. Now widely used throughout to describe a person who commits offences against minors, and it has also been claimed that the use of the word itself derives from Geoffrey Chaucer's *General Prologue* of *The Canterbury Tales*, previously 'nones' turned to 'nonce' in the 1884 publication. Nonetheless, Lang passed through the gates of the Victorian hospital being placed onto an assessment ward, a easy pathway through cushy hospital again for another patient who damn well deserved a cold cell in a prison.

Those whom work inside Broadmoor tell us they do not judge people or their crimes or the reasons for having a bed there. They give different stories to what we expect the patients to be or look like. We are often told , 'He was tall with a squeaky voice not what you imagine after reading their case notes…they do not look scary or intimidating…would I trust them maybe not but who am I to judge them. Never turn your back or trust them.' Lang only had one goal in Broadmoor to have the life that he would not get in the mainstream penal system that was 'feet up and stay comfy'. He was in no doubt what and why he was placed in Broadmoor for a child killer does not fair very well inside prison, always under constant threat of violence towards them along with food being tampered with, or the 'slip-up' on the floor in the shower block followed by an unexpected shaving accident. Today's hospital is there to treat those who suffer mentally not for picking up the pieces the prison system does not want to handle. Settling in takes getting used to and the 'I have my own room' routine. Lang took up writing to those women who seem to think that a bad boy inside Broadmoor is the caring thing to do. Unless you actually know why they are in there we cannot think of anything more stupid than believing that those inside during this dark era were super-sweet and all things nice. Lang had many female pen pals so much so that many visited him inside the red brick walls of the hospital. He had one woman who became close to him during the letters culminating in visits from a middle-aged woman from Southampton. You would think that the hospital security procedures would be strict but clearly not in this case. We all know the *Great Escape* film that has the iconic music score by artist Elmer Bernstein, perhaps Lang had that tune whistling round inside his head. No tunnel option that would have taken longer than the Second World War to dig, mind you the security was far more lapse in the hospital than the Stalag, so anything was possible. A hacksaw and extra blades was smuggled in wrapped was taken in by the woman from Southampton. Another woman managed to smuggle in a rope yes, a rope, not a short one either. The escape attempt was foiled by staff who found the items in Langs room. A court case followed in 1978 where the two women was found guilty of committing a public nuisance and received a suspended sentence each. The outcome was the hospital had to defend itself as to why were the women not searched. The hospital replied.

'He was a paroled patient. Patients on parole are allowed to see their guests on the terraces at the hospital and are not under the strict surveillance.' One fact remains the equipment was detected, and they say the precautions were adequate. Lang's lame excuse was, '…she was in love with me…I was going to hand over the rope to gain the Doctor's trust.' Perhaps with a 'Here, Doc, I was practising the Indian rope trick as part of my rehabilitation, I deliberately had it so you could find it and presume I am trustworthy.'

Some might ask how can a child killer be rehabilitated, or the likes of Sutcliffe, Brady and Rose West change their ways? You release them and they do not go unnoticed on the outside. Lang, on the other hand is not well known by the public along with changing his name he is now even more obscure. One thing is for sure he knew what he was doing so I believe the excuse of diminished responsibility was a con by this man and his legal team, so let's look back at the trial. Lang had previous for sexual assault on young girls and served prison time for those offences. So, what makes him now mentally unfit? Lang played the hospital not just a quick game but the long game. Not happy with the foiled escape attempt he decided he outstayed his welcome at Broadmoor and needed another burst of freedom. Setting up another pen pal, but not having luck with persuading the new lady to pop along to the local hardware store for essentials like a hacksaw or rope, this time he had to do it all on his own. The walls at the time were getting additional security measures built and were supported by scaffolding. Soon we will learn that someone had done a bunk to Holland after Lang. Did Lang and Reeve plan the double escape within weeks of each. The similarities between the escapes being that both used tools both and used women pen pals. Rope and hack saws or tools, were they on the same ward it seems that they were. Would Reeve have colluded with a child killer? Seeing the chance Lang again cut through bars on the room window, this time obtaining a hack saw through a workshop in the hospital unused though in his escape. Broadmoor has always considered itself high security and yet a child killer found a weak point in the system. Lang took a chance by finding his way to the weakest point, scaffolding that was erected to build the new part that was finished in 1982. Climbing the south-facing scaffold Lang made his way along the red bricked wall and jumped. Crack! He's had broken the left ankle but undeterred by the pain Lang hopped off towards Sandhurst, the little-known place that has the officer's college where Bernard Montgomery 11th November 1887 to 24th March 1976, Field Marshall 1st Viscount Montgomery of Alamein, KG, GCB, DSO, PC DL nicknamed Monty once learned his military know-how.

The day of the escape is a familiar one to me. As a child of thirteen I remember the siren that morning and everyone going into a panic. A child killer was on the loose police sirens, roadblocks along with much activity. Bracknell was built on roundabouts, and one could see police stationed at various points effectively cutting off all road routes out. But canny Lang had bolted into the woods taking an easterly direction. The heinous Jimmy Savile requested he helped in the search and was seen out in the woods assisting the police. Schools now on alert and possibly every child at risk so no chances are taken.

Lang headed towards Blackwater in Surrey, a short distance but on foot this 12.3 mile trek involves thick woods and wading through mud. Realising that no one will harbour a sex killer Lang took to finding refuge. Distinctive curly light-coloured hair and hobbling along, he stood out. At 19 London Road, Blackwater, 'The Red Lion' public house - now 'Mr Bumble' – dates from the time of King VI and I James Charles Stuart of Scotland (1566-1625) who ordered that the heraldic Red Lion of Scotland must be displayed on all buildings of importance including public houses. As an aside, the A30 road which runs 284 miles from Hounslow to Land's End, highwaymen used this road to gain their fortunes with many coming to a swinging end hanging from the end of a rope. Two women were inside the pub so Lang took a chance and burst in through the door demanding that both ladies sat down and keep quiet. The door was bolted, and he made sure every other door was locked too. Lang stood no chance of making it any further for a broken ankle and lack of help would only enable him to sit it out for a few hours with two hostages. Little did the two women know of his previous history and Lang was not in any mood to tell them. A request for painkillers and the top up of a gin and tonic was going to ease the pain. Finally, Lang could take no more, hopping across the road Lang phoned 999 from a phone box and asked for the police. Blue lights and sirens came from every direction while he stood outside hands in the air shouting 'I am in pain help me.' Quickly bundled to the ground screaming in pain Lang begged the police he be taken to the hospital at Frimley Park. Then, once back inside the Broadmoor Hospital the 'All Clear' blared out across local areas from the thirteen satellite sirens. The time was 11.30 pm, a relief for the locals. Lang was then moved into an open prison, having by Broadmoor standards, been cured?

Lang changed his name and is currently out there somewhere amongst the population after release during the late 1990s. There were two escapes within weeks of each other some even say he colluded with our next patient. Did Lang and Reeve hatch it together or did the women they wrote to know something?

And did you know that... ...a year before Lang had escaped, the shops in Great Hollands, Bracknell, about a mile and a bit from Broadmoor had a strange incident. A man was outside the local newsagents approaching school children asking them if they wanted to buy a watch. Probably a flash Casio - the one with a calculator – oh, the 80s were so advanced back then, but the unsuspecting children had no idea that the man was an escaped patient. Close to the local junior and infant school the man proceeded to accost people begging for money. Eventually Broadmoor sirens were heard, children scattered, parents screamed and teachers in the school hurried everyone along. The man casually strolled along to J. Pope Chemist and stood outside while the pharmacist called the police. Soon after the cops arrived a scuffle broke out and the man was detained. It scared me as being a nine-year-old in the local junior school it was close, but us kids get excited, so it was the talk of the day for weeks to come. It transpired that Alan Reeve had been on the run for two hours before Broadmoor even noticed that he was missing. All clear sirens blared out and the place returned to normal not for long though - Reeve would escape again.

***

Alan Patrick Reeve.

No Olde Worlde pub sing-alongs in this chapter, moreover, there is most often nothing unusual about a person's name or anything that alerts you to how intelligent some are - others born stupid. However, this chapter examines a man who eventually wrote a book himself; studied sociology and qualified as a lawyer. Furthermore, many assume that those who end up in Broadmoor are raving lunatics, psychopaths or totally untreatable in mainstream hospitals or prisons, so Broadmoor, has without, often become a dumping ground for those deemed unsuitable for any other type of institution. The subject of this chapter, Alan Reeve, was also considered by Charles Bronson - now known as Charles Salvador - as the most dangerous man he has ever come across.

Born in 1948, Alan Reeve was the son of a military prison officer whose job took the family all over Europe and into Libya; eventually settling in Winchester their final destination. Reeve had a problem with authority from a young age, committing crimes including theft, shoplifting and robbery. Whether this was to do with a strict upbringing or being moved around and unable to settle we will never know, but a disruptive childhood often bodes ill for youngsters!

In a bizarre incident at the age of nine, Reeve attempted to shoot his father with a revolver; whether it had been in the possession of his father or that he obtained it by other means, no records have been found to support either, nonetheless, Reeve was fascinated with knives and guns. He admitted later that he had shot two dogs then he strangled a cat – this was followed by using an axe on another cat. Aged twelve, Reeve was caught for shoplifting and larceny (theft of personal property). More trouble followed at the age of thirteen when he was convicted for demanding money with menaces, so it seems that Reeve had the intent to move on to commit more serious crimes.

In January 1964, Reeve, now aged 15, was sent to Borstal for theft. Here he entered into a regime that was strictly run by the prison system with an aim to rehabilitate those who strayed onto the wrong side of the tracks. The idea was to separate those under the age of twenty-one, educate and install discipline along with a work ethic now known as a young offenders' prison. Many of us recalled the 1979 movie *Scum* starring the twenty-two-year Raymond 'Ray' Andrew Winstone playing 'Carlin', who the other lads called 'Daddy'. In other words, Carlin was the 'shot-caller' and we even see this in main prisons – even in the TV sitcom *Porridge* with 'Grouty' played by Peter Vaughan. In fact, there was a, earlier 1949 film called *Boys in Brown* staring Richard Attenborough, Jack Warner and Dirk Bogarde. This movie was based on a play written by Reginald Beckwith – a bit tamer than *Scum* but still just as effective for that period: the plot being a teenager sent to serve three years in Borstal for driving a getaway car. Well that's the movie plugs done and dusted, nevertheless, Reeve soon escaped in August 1964; making his way to Colchester, was while staying in local youth hostel he met Roger Barry Jackson who was on a cycling holiday. Reeve took a dislike to Jackson and beat him to death. Reeve later said: '...he stared at me, and I didn't like the look of him.' Reeve hid Jackson's body in Castle Park, then he disappeared taking Jackson's belongings and three postcards that Jackson had intended sending to his parents. Reeve was now on the run, and in a sick bizarre twist he sent the three pre-addressed postcards to Roger's parents with the letters 'DOA' (Dead on Arrival) written on them. Reeve was soon arrested for murder.

The year is now 1964, and Reeve was detained under the mental health act with no time limit given on how long he should remain in an institution. A one-way ticket to Crowthorne in Berkshire was issued and Broadmoor Hospital found him a bed, to once again accept a patient who was considered highly dangerous, and the future would eventually show how dangerous this man really was. What we have to remember back in the 60s through to the late 80s, Broadmoor was an easy option for the court system to place the likes of Reeve for 'The System' was somewhat different from today's standards.

At the end of the previous chapter we noted that in November 1965 Reeve managed under the noses of the staff in Broadmoor to escape over a wall but he was soon recaptured before the sirens were activated. Then another escape attempt was made in November 1965, but although well-planned it came to nothing.

Anyone who knows through film and books about the drug scene in the 60's will have heard the name 'Purple Heart' – a little tablet that had the effect of bringing one up (also called 'uppers'). During an incident in October 1966, Reeve escaped onto the roof of one of Broadmoor's buildings with 150 of these tablets along with 25 sleeping tablets with him having taken a vast amount of these pills beforehand. If we were to be flippant, just two tabs would be enough to get you on a flight over any building - twenty-five would take you into the stratosphere, all taking that idiom, 'As high as a kite', to completely another level! Nevertheless, he was eventually coaxed down and settled back into the unit.

It has been claimed that Reeve behaved himself and became a model patient, but this is far from the truth. He was constantly at loggerheads with authority and demanded to be moved out of the hospital. Letters were often written to the Home Secretary asking to be moved and demanding better facilities for Reeve always claimed that he was being held as a 'political prisoner', which, of course, in the strict sense, he wasn't.

Perchance, a William Thomas Doyle was being held in Broadmoor at the same time as Reeve and Doyle was given a bed after being found unfit to stand trial for murder. During a 1967 incident in a common room Reeve attacked Doyle and strangled him in front of other patients and it was claimed by Reeve that Doyle had asked him to kill him. Whether it was with murderous intent, or a dislike that had built up between them, no one is ever likely to know, except of course Reeve. He confessed to the murder of Doyle but later claimed he had made the confession up to gain attention of the medical team.

Reeve spent a lot of time writing and receiving correspondence from various women; he was a popular man with the ladies' letter brigade. Tall with wispy blonde hair, slightly balding at the front, heavy rimmed glasses and a hippy look, he could charm the knickers off of any woman to whom he took a fancy. He was also known to spend time in the hospital workshops where patients were encouraged to make use of the facilities to make various items, try their hands at welding, sewing and woodwork. A lot of these items were sold via the hospital shop to the public and money earned from these ventures was often ploughed back into the hospital funds for the use of the patients: a practice, which, it seems, has now unfortunately stopped.

At this point in Reeve's narrative it is right to remember why he has been given a bed in this highly secure facility – because he was diagnosed as being very seriously mentally unhinged, so stark raving bonkers that no mainstream prison would entertain him, that's why. But does he seem insane to you; oh, boy, this man had his wits about him, that's for sure. Highly dangerous but not as mad as the proverbial hatter, indeed, he comes across as being as crafty as a town fox. Put it this way, when they look into a mirror many of Broadmoor's patients think that they are talking to a complete stranger, even Donald Trump or Jesus Christ – the latter which 'The Donald' imagines himself to be. Yes, yes, I am being obtuse here, but at this point my colleague (Christopher Berry-Dee) would like to relate a true incident that happened, a few years ago, so here it is in the first person:

*

'A lady friend of mine had a mental breakdown and had been sectioned; to be placed in 'The Orchards' at St James' Hospital, Portsmouth. I was allowed to visit with her in this secure facility and several times I did, so much so that the staff and shrinks knew who I was and what my career was all about. Indeed, a few of them had even seen me on the television. On one occasion – and for reasons soon to become clear, my last occasion – there I was, immaculate, wearing a smart navy blazer, highly-polished brogues, white shirt, links, and carrying a leather attaché case and, having just spoken to the psychiatrist, I intended to leave – when, guess what, I was stopped by some woman doctor whom it appeared had just sucked a lemon. So, here is the God's truth dialogue pretty much verbatim:'

Doctor:	And where do you think *YOU* are going?
Me:	Home.
Doctor:	Oh, NO you are NOT!
Me:	I have just visited with Miss XXXX and spoken to the psychiatrist.
Doctor:	Yes, a lot of our patients talk to each other and the psychiatrists too. Now go back to your room.
Me:	I'm not Napoleon, you know.
Doctor:	I can see that. You are not wearing his hat.

By this time my patience has expired:

Me: Look, see this lapel pin. It says FBI
                    Behavioral Science Unit. Take a look for
                    God's fuckin' sake!
Doctor: Ah, so you made that in here, did you?
Me: The trouble with clowns like you, you have
                    been around so many mentally ill people for
                    so long you have become as nuts as they are.
                    Now open that door and clear off.

With that, the chief shrink rushed out of his office and opened the door to free me with many, many sincere apologies for having me detained for so long. I never went back.'

So now let's return to Mr. Reeve. Sociology, the study of human behaviour, interactions and patterns of social relationships is not an easy subject to study but for Reeve he *did* study the subject and received a high-level grade during his stay at Broadmoor. The encouragement one gets from the 'system' seemed to work for Reeve, but maybe one gets the impression that this man was telling others he was more intelligent than them – which it could also be argued, in many ways he was.

More letters from admiring women were arriving and during the late 70s Reeve struck up a relationship with a Patricia Ford who started visiting him. Then, during an incident in the workshop circa 1980 Reeve threatened to kill a nurse who he then attacked with a clamp in a fit of rage to cause substantial injuries which required over a hundred stiches. This incident is not well known, however, during the research for this book a member of this nurse's family confirmed that this almost murderous assault did take place.

In 1981 Reeve was up to no good again in planning an escape with the aid of the aforementioned Patricia Ford who organised the escape set-up on the outside. While watching television, Reeve managed to get hold of an aerial – of some substance it seems – and crafted it into a grappling hook. He collected up numerous bed sheets taken from other patients, which beggars' belief that the security was not much up to scratch. It was said at this time by various reports that Reeve was placed under surveillance by a 'Special Watch' hospital official. Now some say those who are held in Broadmoor spend much time hours plotting escapes. 'There's time and there's Broadmoor time', is a phrase often used and still continues to be. Reeve being extremely dangerous and cunning and was using any means to gain the trust of those around him. Indeed, even when Patricia Ford visited, she managed to smuggle in items he could use to help him escape: a hack saw blade was one item along with some scissors she'd brought with it.

We must also remember that during this era passports and documents were easy to obtain. One-year passports were the norm by popping down to a post office showing some ID like a birth certificate, paper driving licence or credit card along with two photos and within ten minutes you had one. Patricia Ford would have organised all of those aspects of the plan, quite obviously so because it *might* have raised suspicions if Reeve had asked staff if he could wander down to the shops in Crowthorne, nipping into Postman's Pat's office while doing so.

During the morning of 9 August 1991, staff checked Reeves room and noticed he was missing. Preferring not to sound the alarm. a search was conducted throughout the hospital. Finally, with Reeves still unaccounted for, the sirens blared out throughout parts of Berkshire for twenty minutes. Roadblocks were set up in parts of Berkshire, Surrey and Hampshire in an attempt to stop and locate him. Reports were issued by radio describing Reeve as six foot in height (1.8 meters), 11 stone (70 kg) in weight, thin with light coloured hair, thin build. The escape itself included bed sheets tied together to form a rope. He had climbed up and over an 18-foot wall using the grappling hook (made from this ariel attached to the sheets. At the time of this escape Broadmoor was having a makeover; new buildings were going up   , scaffolding was everywhere, and the second exterior wall was vulnerable, and this was all used to wily Reeves's advantage and Patricia Ford was waiting on the outside in what was believed to have been a hired car. The route the pair took away from the hospital is unknown, but a trip to one of the cross-channel ferry ports is certain. During the 1980s, the security at ports was not as robust as today. Reeve had a two-hour head start on everyone and certainly enough time to flee to one of the ports – one suspects Portsmouth being the nearest. The nurse who was attacked in Broadmoor the year before was contacted by the police because Reeve had threatened to kill her if he ever got out, so this was taken seriously by the authorities. A police escort was sent to chaperone the family around while they were on holiday in Scotland, little did anyone know that Reeve was leaving the UK. It is also thought in some quarters that Reeve had escaped to prove a point to the authorities that he was capable of leading a normal life after writing to the then Home Secretary, William 'Willie' Whitelaw, and being turned down for release. If the authorities would not release him, he would free himself.

Arriving in France, then travelling into Holland, the country of the clog, dykes with small holes in them and Edam cheese, which according to the brand 'travels well', as did Reeve who was now on the run with his girlfriend Patricia. They made their way to Amsterdam and settled between squats throughout the city. Reeve was never going to change habits or settle down as he kept on claiming in his letters to the authorities in the UK. Shoplifting, stealing, and using savings they had squirreled away, the UK authorities was totally unaware of their whereabouts.

A year had now passed since the escape and still moving from squats to run-down digs, Reeve was in the mood to celebrate his year of freedom and a local liquor shop was the target. He made his way in a car with the intention of stealing whisky and Cointreau, then a small fight broke out when shop staff tried to stop him. The Dutch police were immediately on the scene. Reeve was armed with a pistol and fled to his waiting car, thereafter a 'Sweeny' type of car chase ensued at speed through the canal district of Amsterdam, which ended with a shootout during which Reeve received three gunshot wounds. Two Dutch police officers were injured, and Officer Jaap Honingh was shot dead.

At first, the cops believed Reeve to be a Canadian citizen named 'Steven' or 'Simon Harbison' but they were skeptical about his full identity. Searching the flat Reeve where he was staying, they found an arsenal of weapons: two shotguns; two handguns, ammunition and knives with other 'tools. Police thought Reeves might have been a terrorist, leaving them to scratch their heads and muttering: 'Het is volkomen duidelijk dat hij iets van plan is, maar we weten niet wat', which is along the lines of: 'It's perfectly clear he is up to something, but we don't know what'.

The endgame was nigh. British authorities were alerted along with Interpol to obtain Reeves correct details with a request from the UK for Reeve to be extradited, which was refused by the Dutch as Reeves was charged with murder. Interpol had written to the British authorities saying that if Reeve were found guilty and sentenced under Dutch law, he would probably not be extradited to serve out his life term at Broadmoor. Reeve was remanded to Norgerhaven Prison, Veenhuizen, during which period he allegedly married his partner-in-crime, Patricia Ford. At trial, he was found guilty of manslaughter and sentenced to fifteen-years and returned to prison to serve his time.

During Reeve's imprisonment he obtained a degree studying political science from the University of Leiden during 1988. Reeve still not content with the situation of being held and still regarding himself as a political prisoner attempted to free himself, again unsuccessfully. The Dutch authorities moved Reeve to the more secure Hague Penitentiary Institution at Scheveningen. This seemed to upset Reeve even more and he acted by going on hunger strike for 54 days. Now resigned to serving his time and with plenty of time on his hands he took to writing a thesis: *'The Creation and Preservation of Consciousness.'* Between 1988 and 1992 Reeve did behave himself taking up further education and studying to become a lawyer in the Dutch system. He became very adept at the subject and obtained an extremely high level of study. The Dutch prison reform group known as 'Coornhert Liga' began working with Reeve – the equivalent of 'Howard League for Penal Reform' group in the UK. And it seems that this type of interaction was having some effect on Reeve himself, so could a prison sentence in the UK have been a more appropriate course of action in the first place?

Ten years had been served and under Dutch law Reeve was eligible for parole. The UK government requested Reeve be extradited back to Britain and this was refused by the Dutch. A year later, in 1993, a further request by the UK for Reeve to be extradited was granted, however, Reeve was nowhere to be found – he had gone on the run once again. Totally under the radar Reeve managed to evade detection from the Dutch, UK and Interpol for two years. The Dutch press questioned why this man was allowed to conduct his own plea, papers, and they also reported how Reeve became suited for a position on the Coonhort League Board given his theoretical and knowledge of the Dutch prison system. It was during this time that Patricia Ford and Reeve parted company.

Two more years had passed. It's now 1995 with Reeve having made his way to The Republic of Ireland. Cork was the next port of call, and for the international fugitive into the glamorous job of typesetting for a women's poetry circle along with joining the local knitting group. After all the years spent on the run and knocking people off, Alan Reeve, now calling himself Harry, was finally doing something that we can all relate to. The Cork women's circle must have held some mysterious attraction to him going from high-speed car chases, climbing walls along with the thrill of being on the run. Along with the ancient art of knitting and sitting in a room with all different colours of fluffy balls of wool, maybe the relaxing element crept in and the fugitive was finally finding his vocation in life.

Finding love again with one Anne Murphy and her son, still moving round Cork to various addresses then finally settling in Cork, UK authorities got a tip off from the Irish Garda who were themselves tipped off by the public in 1997. Extradition papers were sent over and an arrest was made in April of the same year. Reeve had made a bargain agreeing to the extradition after that it was alleged he was told that his sentence would be commuted after his: '…good behaviour over a long period of time'. Reeve never opposed the extradition, this time finally accepting that he had to return to Broadmoor as he had never been officially released or finished the sentence originally handed down to him. The hospital required that this be the case, so he was returned for assessment. Bracknell Magistrates' court was set for the hearing. Handcuffed to two Broadmoor staff and attending in green shirt, red blazer and black trousers, slightly balding hair along with glasses that reacted to light. Reeve stood in the dock. He said nothing and made no objection when ordered to return to Broadmoor. A heavy police presence was throughout the court and the surrounding area. Reeve, now fifty-years-old, and who had been on the run for sixteen years, was finally back in Broadmoor. The 'All-Clear' sirens should have been sounded throughout Berkshire as the patient had been recaptured, but someone forgot to push the button.

Reeve was assessed again by various doctors over the next five months, and it was said that he no longer posed a threat to society. In October 1997, Reeve was released having served his time. He sailed back to Ireland, the knitting circle, to Ann Murphy now his wife along with five children.

Alan Reeve lived out his life writing, knitting, and typesetting for the ladies of Cork. Indeed, his story is one for the movies; containing all that is required: murder; escape; being a fugitive along with knitting, he died of cancer surrounded by his loving supportive family in Ireland on Tuesday, 12 July 2016.

***

Michael Gordon Peterson aka Charles Ali Ahmed aka Charles 'Charlie' Bronson, Charles Arthur Salvador aka Lord Charles Salvador.

'When I get bad heads, I'm unsafe, unstable – but I know I'm not
a psychopath. I've lived with psychos. I know what makes them tick.
I'm different…I do have a conscience and I do feel guilt. But I
will never ask for forgiveness for attempting to kill the
paedophile [John] White I've never harmed women or children
and I despise any man that does.'

Bronson: as Michael Gordon Peterson.

There are few things more disastrous-prone than the designs of petty criminals who have aspirations above their mental abilities; influenced by what they read – if they can *actually* read – or see on TV, these over-ambitious mediocrities consider that they are capable of emulating the exploits of those whom they perceive to be eminently more successful than they themselves have been. Fueled by the wrong motives, often greed or revenge, they lay plans which are ill thought out and, almost always, destined to end in failure – enter stage left and into the limelight, one…um…now what name do we actually call this thug? Yep, Peterson will suffice!

Of course, as you dear reader will have already instantly noted, this guy likes different 'names' does he not? Born in Luton, 6 December 1952, and forgetting his birth surname – as he seems to have done – he self-adopted the name of 'Ali Ahmed' and God only knows which *real* Ali Ahmed, or it could have been 'Ali Abbas al-Ahmed aka Ali AL Ahmed' for all we know. Then came the famous American actor: Charles 'Charlie' Bronson (1921-2003), who, incidentally, had also changed his name – he was born' Charles Dennis Buchinsky', to become cast in roles as of cops, gunfighters, or vigilantes in revenge-orientated plots – the latter our homegrown Charles Bronson revels in. Up next is 'Charles Salvador'; nicking that from the great artist Spanish artist Salvador Dalí (1904-1989), who incidentally considerably shortened his name for he was born…wait for it…'Salvador Domingo Felipe Jacinto Salvador Dalí I Doménech', to later become 'Ist Marquess of Dalí de Púbol'. However, it seems that becoming a mere Marquess was not quite up Charlie's Street, so his family bought their notorious criminal a piece of Scottish land near Galloway for the princely sum of £79.00 (not sure if this included VAT) and the Proclamation, now laminated in his cell confirms that Charlie: '…may henceforth and in perpetuity be known by the style and title of Lord and shall hereafter be known as Lord Charles Arthur Salvador.' So, make of that if you will, moreover, let us go on a journey with one of the most confused, dangerous, intelligent and sometimes funny inmates/patients the system has ever dealt with.

He has almost as many name changes than a local TV cable company, to travel virtually through many of the prisons in the UK from the Isle of Wight to Scotland. Confusing himself, along with me and you, the reader, by the time this chapter finishes we will *all* be scratching our heads.

'He's a lovely man.

Paula Williamson: Peterson's wife on Bronson.

Charlie's exploits include and not limited to: hostage taking; armed robbery x 2; wounding with intent, criminal damage, grievous bodily harm; false imprisonment x 3; blackmail; threatening to kill; assaulting police officers, prison staff and the occasional prisoner and hospital patient, all mixed in with his rooftop viewing hobby and the fun he can have with exercise while in a cell, this man is a mind-bending puzzle of multiple personalities and behavioural traits that will leave us all dizzy.

He's changed his religion, married a Fatema Saira Rehman in 2001, divorced in 2005, married an Irene Kelsey in 1972, divorced her in 1975, then the actress, Paula Williamson, in 2017, and talks to anyone who will lend him an ear, including animals, too. And yes, they even made the 2008 movie *Bronson*, about him starring Tom Hardy who played 'Charles Peterson'. There are more documentaries and YouTube postings one can shake a stick at, you simply could not make this up if one tried and, for this reason: the movie Peterson name change came after his stay at Broadmoor, so we will stick with that.

Although 'His Lordship' has never killed anyone, the media seem to consider him one of the most dangerous psychiatric hospitals' patients and prison inmates in the UK system; having served more time on the inside than out, causing hundreds of thousands of pounds worth of damage throughout. Some of us might think he could have made many a good roofing business succeed. He has certainly kept the authorities in work for a number of years along with building companies and suppliers. The media refer to Peterson – now Lord Salvador – as a thug, Britain's most dangerous violent prisoner that has ever walked the wings of the penal system: Broadmoor, Rampton and Ashworth psychiatric hospitals have all had the misfortune to have housed him along with the highest security mainstream prisons. At the time of writing, he is held at HMP Woodhill, Milton Keynes, in a close supervision unit for the safety of others. Furthermore, when I say that someone takes the roof off a place I mean it as in a theatrical term or a big show, yet this man literally did take some of the roof off Broadmoor Hospital, the tiles and wood along with masonry. During his stay here he caused no end of trouble for the authorities along while keeping the local papers interested in the hospital. They say that there is no such thing as bad publicity, do we not?

Born to Mother Eira and Father Joe Peterson, along with two other brothers, growing up in the Bedfordshire area until a teenager before, aged thirteen, moving to Elsmere Port in Cheshire, he was not a troublemaker when young and was a very bright at school, but one thing upset Peterson - the school bullies. It was the move to Cheshire when he started to get into trouble being the member of a gang of four who were into robbery: once getting a severe reprimand from a juvenile court for theft. It was during this era Peterson started to enjoy fighting, absenteeism from school was a common trait. Not happy, he returned to Luton, which he has always regarded as his own town to take up a job in Tesco. This effort lasted two weeks then he attacked a manager and was sacked. Various other jobs came and went including a short stint as a brickie's hod carrier. His first term of incarceration was at Risley Remand Centre for committing criminal damage after a row with his first girlfriend's father. Another job, as a furniture remover, mixed with regular fights during the evenings followed, then, not happy with the petty crime Peterson moved up a level – stealing a lorry resulting in fines and more probation.

In 1974, Peterson, now aged 22, was convicted of armed robbery and was awarded a seven-year sentence at HMP Liverpool (formerly Walton Gaol) along with a stint in the punishment block for attacking two inmates without being provoked. In 1975 he was 'shipped out' to HMP Hull, and after refusing prison work, he smashed up a workshop following a row with a 'screw'. He was injected with the sedative chlorpromazine, which made him violently ill, and an extra six-months 'bird' was added to the sentence. In and out of solitary confinement, he then attacked John Henry Gallagher with a glass jug. Nine more months were added to his sentence then he was transferred to HMP Leeds (known locally as Armley Gaol).

Transporting Peterson around the penal system was an event in itself, being chained down to prison vans' floors, kept alone and at a distance from anyone in close proximity he was considered so dangerous. His time in HMP Wandsworth was not uneventful for the other prisoners on the wings with his attempt to poison an inmate in the next cell resulting in another move. At HMP Parkhurst on the Isle of Wight in 1976 he met his idols, the Kray twins. Not happy with the way things were turning out or the treatment he was receiving he started causing problems again, so he was moved again to HMP Wandsworth. Deciding that an escape was the only option for him, he took to using various tools in an attempt to dig himself out and was immediately thrown into isolation for four months. Another inmate had informed the Governor of the escape attempt, thereafter, Peterson attacked the prisoner who had, in prison slang, 'grassed him up.

Time moved slowly on with Peterson being moved about more often than a knight on a chessboard. Briefly visiting Ashworth high security psychiatric hospital, Merseyside, then Rampton Hospital, Nottinghamshire, Peterson would claim that they were 'shitholes' and 'unfit to hold a nut case' like himself. Finally, a move to what he called was the elite of the elite, Broadmoor, where he was supposedly to have said before the move, '…here I come. I've won the fucking lottery'. This burst of elation was possibly because Ronnie Kray was there and Peterson classed him as a close and personal friend. However, as might be expected, Peterson's stay was going to be eventful.

> 'I had to sit in a day room at Rampton Hospital surrounded by sex killers, rapists and child slayers. I listened to their madness. I smelt their madness. I knew that either I had to go, or I'd end up completely mad myself. I decided to kill White.'
>
> Peterson.

According to the press, 1978 was the year the Berkshire village of Crowthorne was to gain the most dangerous inmate the system has ever dealt with, however, after a month he was returned to Rampton apparently due to an adverse reaction to the drugs administered in Broadmoor, but Peterson only had a brief stay at Rampton after an attempt to murder a child sex killer, John White; a 'slimy rat with evil all over his face', who had killed a little girl after he had sexually assaulted her:

> 'My plan was simple. If I murdered the monster, I'd go back to court and be sent back to a proper prison to serve out my life sentence. I thought I would be doing society a big favour by topping him. For a couple of days, I plotted the monster's departure. Strangulation was the only way. I was difficult because I always had two white coats with me. There was only one real chance – to grab him in the day room. I sat right behind him while we were watching TV – then I whipped off my tie and wrapped it around the pervert's neck. I pulled as tight as I could.'

Without seeming to be cynical – and no doubt some of our readers will vehemently disagree with me – our 'Charlie' appears to be 'bad' rather than 'mad' as in being 'stark raving off-the-wall bonkers'. To begin with, his recollection of the events is extremely lucid, his grammar is good and not of a style penned by a man drugged up the eyeballs and spending most of his time chained to a wall. And, in his own way he's quite articulate, as he continues:

> 'I was killing a man before their very eyes and getting away with it. His whole body was shaking like he was having a fit. I heard his death rattle. His face had turned blue, his eyes were bulging, and his tongue hung down his chin. This monster was on his way out and I felt so happy. He was getting off lightly for what he had done to that little girl.
>
> 'Then the white coats were on my back, punching and trying to prise my hands free of the tie I was winding round his neck. I was shouting, screaming and laughing. I was now completely mad!
>
> 'I heard shouts for oxygen and people running – but most of all I could hear my own laughter as they dragged me away.'

According to Peterson, they slung him in a cell and cut off his clothes with scissors, they injected him. 'I was still shouting and laughing,' he said, adding: 'I've killed the monster. I've killed him!'

He asked to be charged with attempted murder, but his psychiatrist said that Peterson was too mentally disturbed to stand trial. 'So, I was now Rampton's Public Enemy No.1', he has written.

Of course, we could take some of this with a pinch of salt, but then it seems that he took a liking to 'lunatic' who thought that he was 'The Elephant Man'. 'I gave him a bun,' says Peterson, 'because elephants love buns'.

'Another thought that he was Pope,' recalls Peterson, 'and he kept blessing us all. In the end I grabbed his throat and head-butted him. Not a nice thing to do – but there you have it, I nutted the Pope,' he adds with a wry sense of perfectly sane humour.

Keen to show that he is not a psychopath, Peterson says that he also '…felt a lot of compassion for a man called Hutchy, His neck was all twisted – it hung down on his right shoulder and he was forever staring at the ceiling,' adding, '…he lost his marbles many times. The saddest day was when his mother made her annual visit. He was so excited that he went funny and smashed both his arms through a window and tore them open. His mother had to see him in the infirmary. This, to me, was so tragic.'

It all rather sounds like something far worse than the movie, *One Flew Over the Cuckoo's Nest*, but then there was a 'John Boy'. Peterson says that he couldn't talk or do anything for himself, and he had no teeth.' So do we see a psychopath in Peterson here –I think not, for he adds: '…every morning John used to run out of his cell, covered in his own mess. He would run to the bath and jump in. One of us had to scrub him and dress him, then walk him back to the day room to be strapped in his chair'.

The reader might be wondering how is it that such a highly-dangerous psychiatric patient who had almost killed another man, has become almost a carer for a mentally-ill person, for Peterson adds: 'He'd sit there making animal sounds and I'd pat him on the head to calm him down. I'd never felt more sorry for another human being,' despite the fact: '...he attacked me several times but I never once retaliated. I felt so sad for him that I used to buy a bag of chocolates every week just to give him the soft ones.'

Peterson says that he spent half of his seventeen months at Rampton in 'seclusion'. I was even denied a pen to write a letter. The system was all set to destroy me. The only way out was to do something so violent that I'd be transferred back to prison – which seems somewhat contradictory with him having come out of seclusion and almost reformed as an ad hoc nursing aide, which seems a good move in the right treatment direction, maybe?

Yet, Mr Peterson is, indeed a contradiction in so many confusing ways. He decided to smash a nurse's head with a lump of concrete. 'I know now it was wrong to take it out on an innocent nurse, but I was a desperate man. Outside the unit was a concrete shop that made paving stones.'

According to Peterson, he made a deal with an 'inmate', which again rather flips over the generally accepted 'patient/s' tag, does it not? 'I'd give him five packets of fags for a good piece of concrete. But he grassed me up. I denied it but I was back in seclusion.' Five packets of cigarettes in a patient's possession in the highly secure psychiatric hospital is a non-starter for all sorts of reasons, so there could be some gilding the lily going on here. Nevertheless, he says that he was called in to see the 'doc' and told that Rampton could do no more for him. 'So, I was on my way to Broadmoor, my home for the next five years'. God only knows what would have happened if he'd bumped into Jimmy Saville (the subject of a chapter to come) – probably have ripped the obsequious paedophile's head off might have been a starter for ten.

Broadmoor was in the era of not being very well received by the media in general. It has been reported that electro-compulsive therapy, drugs, and beatings were common, or so it was said by many on the inside. Lax security was also an issue. Peterson always maintained Broadmoor was the elite and held the elite. Nonetheless, after having a brief introduction to the regime all Peterson wanted was to be with his old friend Ronnie Kray with whom he had built up a close relationship with at HMP Parkhurst. Peterson could not believe the difference between the prison system and the hospital system – the latter back then with little restriction on food or the clothing one could wear. Cupboards full of sweets, chocolate and cigarettes were a common hoard according to Peterson and his mate Ronnie had it all.

Peterson was feeling that those in Broadmoor were mad and totally lost the plot as he would say – and he might well have been correct on that note, too. It was said by him that some patients even believed that spiders spoke to them, and he was even told by one patient that 'my spider will kill you.' Shaking his head on many occasions. Peterson says that he even found two men having a 'session in a bathroom' while he was shaving: 'there's a special type of loon in this place, and they even bum each other,' was his non-PC observation.

They say that a leopard never changes its spots, and this truism can be readily applied to Mr Peterson. According to him he, '…ended up in Norfolk Ward, which housed the 'Cream of the Madmen'. 'One guy had decapitated his mother and was arrested on a bus with her head inside a shopping bag', he tells us.

Peterson took a particular dislike to bespectacled bigmouth Gordon Robinson. Not a cheery chap one might invite around for a party for aged 27 he had suffocated 14-year-old John Arthur Roebuck during sex. The body was discovered in Robinson's car after he went to buy a can of petrol and he appeared to not have been aware that the lad was now as dead as the proverbial Dodo. In mitigation, he claimed to have suffered from epilepsy all of which had impaired his responsibility. He was convicted of non-capital murder, sentenced to a full life tariff to end up in Broadmoor. For further reading on this case (No. DPP 2/2644) one can submit a FOI request to the National Archives, although there is an 'Extended Closure Order' in place; the opening date being 1 January 2058, so one will have to wait a long while for a reply.

Times would certainly change for Peterson in Broadmoor. Often given drugs, placed in a room without furniture, placed in a straitjacket and subjected to electro-compulsive therapy and beaten up by staff on a least six occasions, he now realized this was a system he could no longer beat. His pal, Ronnie Kray, had been placed into another ward that had more freedom, more responsibility to roam free around the ward and have one's own door key - unlike Peterson who was still subjected to lockdown at certain times.

On 21 May 1981, Peterson climbed up onto one of Broadmoor's roofs via the loft space. Almost out of scene from the TV sitcom Porridge, Superintendent Dr Udwin tried to coax his errant patient down and received a slate flung in his direction as a reward. It took Ronnie Kray to talk him down.

Peterson sent to the segregation block again, under 24-hour watch supervision along with the six man unlock and lock-up procedure. Behaving, but missing Kray and the relationship they had built up, started taking its toll on his state of mind. Spiders were the only company Peterson had, along with the chats with the arachnids including offering one out for a fight. Is it the system doing the damage, or is it the damage doing the system? United again with Kray on another ward and the bond becoming stronger the two re-kindled their blooming relationship bonded by multiple cups of tea.

Peterson appears to be oblivious to whether he is coming or going so let us try to get back on track. The years are moving on he is plodding along with Broadmoor life; having group sessions where they all sit in a circle discussing each and everyone's problems. One-on-one talks with psychiatrists and regular visits from his parents, often seeing Violet Kray along with Charlie in the visiting hall, taking a more avid interest in their lives than his own. He was often seen down on the football pitch watching the home team playing football – for some strange reason Broadmoor United never played away – with Ronnie Kray often accompanying Peterson to watch the match. Of some anecdotal amusement, he gave up watching the matches when Kray – who was gay – was alleged to have said: '…that number ten has a nice arse'. And, as your author recalls:

> 'That 70s and 80s era, what a laugh that was created for some, especially me. It was during a weekend and my dad played football for a local team. The game was at Broadmoor; eleven players were counted in along with the manager and three others. It was during the game an extra player had turned up and was rushed straight through without being logged in with security. The game ended and on exit there was one extra that could not be accounted for. They kept my father inside Broadmoor overnight. So, let us just say, eventually the next morning upon his home coming started the old police interview routine by one of the famous housewife's detectives

that every household seemed to have had. I fell about laughing as my mother carried on, but it all fizzled out after eleven years of intense debate and pain and finally death.'

Is Peterson really mad, or did he know what he was doing by fooling the system for an easier life along with the hospital regime which is much easier than a mainstream prison. A man who committed a crime yet, when incarcerated, created more trouble forcing the system to add more time to his already lengthy sentence. Peterson maintained the persona that he was given Britain's hardest prisoner originally (self-proclaimed), but in Broadmoor things are different. You are a patient and the nurses along with doctors decide who you are and you do not pick and choose your treatment. In the 70s and 80s the PC brigade did not have a say unlike today when a patient's excrement is even scrutinized along with the toilet paper.

Of course, it seems that Peterson was opting for an easier life along with the dangerous and unpredictable who bumbled around the wards of the hospital. Alan Reeve came to Peterson's attention sharing a day room with him Peterson acknowledged Reeve as the most dangerous he ever met, considering how bad Peterson had been and could get as it took his whim. The life inside the secure hospital gave him more freedom than the prison system, a life of riley as some would say. That old phrase comes from a popular song of the 1880s: 'Is that Mr Reilly?' by Pat Rooney; describing what it is a hero would do if he came into money. Nevertheless, this era of the hospital's dark history sent a message to those on the outside, laying about all day getting up late, eating watching the four channels on the TV, along with the many visits keeping the patients occupied. Was this the truth or not…was the treatment that the patients were allegedly getting have any effect on their mental health?

Peterson spent many a day on drugs and away with the fairies, so how could this be having any mental health benefits for him let alone anyone else? Now needing to vent his anger, we will recall that Gordon Robinson was Peterson's target in the communal area – a silk tie was used to strangle the man. The tie ripped and this more-or-less prevented Peterson from murdering the fellow patient. After this incident Peterson became depressed. His spirits were given a lift when Kray arranged a visit from boxer Terry Downs. The high that followed did not last long. Segregation was the only option for this notorious patient and unhappy with his lot he took to the roof of the hospital on two more occasions – once spending a week up in the air before being finally being coaxed down by his brother. Anyone who has ever walked round the outside of the hospital will appreciate the stunning vast views on offer from the high point of the area, especially in the Autumn. It was estimated that he had caused one million pounds worth of damage in total: a vast sum in those days, in today's money one could triple that.

Can one even begin to imagine this regime inside Broadmoor: stalkers who follow you around, and even Peterson had one on the inside? A fellow patient begging him to beat him up and cause as much pain as he could. 'Go on I know you can do it, give me your best,' was allegedly heard by one security officer inside the hospital. Constantly being followed and pestered by the unnamed patient but never carrying out the deed, Peterson was by far the most popular patient, and he also attracted a large fan club on the outside with even letters along with female underwear allegedly being sent in used, or unused.

The name changes to Bronson came about *via* a suggestion by Kray to bolster the image of the now bare-knuckle fighter after release, which only lasted weeks. Now back inside prison due to a relapse while shopping for an engagement ring – we mean armed robbery, time moved on and a new hobby was painting, then another name change this time to Salvador in honour of the painter. Lord Salvador who he is now known by due to his son purchasing a land title in Scotland.

'Can the Ethiopian change his skin, or the leopard his spots?
Then may ye also do good that are accustomed to do evil.

Jeremiah 13:23 (*King James Version*)

Yep, okay Mr 'Jerry' Jeremiah, but we gotta tell ya that the British criminal justice system and legions of mental health doctors and nurses and caregivers have been trying your suggestion to do good for Lord Salvador over decades. But it just doesn't work 'Jerry'. So, us real folk must ask, what will become of this recently hatched 'Lord Salvador?'

To start to answer this question we know as fact that he is an institutionalized recidivist thru and thru. Recidivism is measured by criminal acts that result in re-arrest, reconviction or return to prison with or without a new sentence following a person's release. A more PC term for incarceration – be it in a secure psychiatric hospital or a mainstream prison – is 'Incapacitation' *inter alia*: referring to the effect of a sanction to stop people from committing crime by removing the offender from the community. We can also call this a 'specific deterrence', being the terminology used to denote whether a sanction stops people from committing further crime once the sanction has been imposed or completed. Finally, we turn to 'rehabilitation'. This refers to the extent to which a programme is implicated in the reduction of crime by socially 'repairing' the individual in some way by addressing his or her needs or deficits.

There are those thousands of Lord Salvador's supporters and diehard fans who campaign for his release; arguing that he is a good man; a changed man, a reformed man, a guy would never again hurt a fly. But look what happens when the system does trust him and releases him - out he goes and commits armed robbery so that he can buy his fiancée a ring.

So what if our Lord Salvador has often been very protective and caring towards other prison inmates and some patients in Broadmoor? This amounts to nothing more than a hill of beans, does it not? Who really cares one bit if many convicts and the mentally ill think that he's a born again 'Sanctus Salvator' [note the similarity between Salvador here]? Maybe to them he *is* an idol, someone they can admire and worship, but if they think this in their unhinged minds, maybe to those of us living in the 'real world', one where elephants do *not* fly, lead balls do *not* bounce and fairies do *not* reign supreme, then he might be construed as a false god; a totally mixed up manipulating individual, all muscle and brawn, albeit with some artistic and poetic talent to give him his due. But, you see, he has been given chance after chance, help after help at the taxpayers' mega huge financial expense to reform and learn from his past ways. C'mon guys and gals, this is a guy who thinks that Ronnie Kray is worth sucking up to – not something that any right-minded person would want to boast about to be sure.

There is also no doubt that he is a hard-case incorrigible; pathologically totally incapable of being corrected or reformed; difficult to control or manage; one, therefore, can say that there is an irreversible 'mental construction flaw', and as time has proven all too well, any attempt to amend it would cause a complete collapse – in his non-obedient recalcitrant case resorting to committing acts of extreme violence when things don't go the way he demands or suits him best.

Does this self-styled Lord care about his cost to the public purse – your hard-earned taxes – or even the terror and physical harm he has caused to countless people over the decades – no, he does not. He does not give two fucks except whine and complain about his time behind bars like some overgrown baby whose toys have been thrown out of its cot.

Did Broadmoor serve him well? Yes, the hospital did have its faults, some very serious lapses of security and this is an undeniable fact, too. But guess where M'lud is right now. Nope, not in his castle out on some desolate moor, shooting grouse and toe-sucking, backside-sniffing members of the Royalty as all those Lords and Ladies are wantonly inclined to do. The whole bunch is a freeloading, ermine wearing waste of space – titled ponces to be sure! Yet, our Lord Salvador wants to be amongst them, except he can't. Bless his multi-faceted Dr Jekyll and Mr. Hyde persona, he is now banged up in HMP Woodhill, Milton Keynes, with Broadmoor Hospital staff celebrating seeing back of him with the popping of balloons, blowing the obligatory plastic glittering party whistles and horns and bowls of different types of nuts scattered about…ouch, that was honestly an unintended pun…all singing 'Auld Lang Syne'.

Lord Charles Salvador sent a letter after a request was sent from the author asking if he wished to add anything to this chapter. He replied:

'I'm now closer to freedom than I have ever been in 30 yrs. exciting times.

Unfortunately, it be on a very secure release police involved, security, probation a hostel and a tag surveillance 24/7.

But it will still be heaven to me; "My first call will be a fry up in a greasy spoon ".

Then a session in a boxing gym a good spar.

My time is arse twitching near,

Signed along with a scruffy spider.

Ps: so many believed I was buried …even me at one time.

Never swim in treacle!'

***

Peter William Sutcliffe aka 'The Yorkshire Ripper'.

'Killing prostitutes had become an obsession with me. I could not stop. It was
like a drug.'

Peter Sutcliffe (1946-2020)

Thus far we have come across some of the most dangerous totally unstable of
patients, not only to themselves but other patients and staff alike. However,
there many patients who do conform to the hospital's regime and 'The
Yorkshire Ripper' was amongst them.

Surrounded by controversy contempt and utter hatred, along with
being attacked by other main prison inmates and hospital patients, Sutcliffe
hoodwinked the system for years leading the authorities, who should have
known better, into believing that he was schizophrenic, vulnerable and
needing attention or being the centre of attention. Having murdered thirteen
women in the late 70s early 80s along with attacking several prostitutes, there
is a belief he killed even more.

Sutcliffe has been written about more times than one can count; along with TV documentaries, magazines coupled with the theories of whodunit, whatdunit and where dunit, he is probably the most talked about UK serial killer we have ever encountered. Moreover, Broadmoor's dark history does not get any blacker than when the hospital gave the Yorkshire Ripper a bed, especially when he struck up a friendship with the most heinous individual to not face prosecution – Sir James Wilson Vincent Savile OBE KCSG, an English DJ, television, and radio personality who hosted BBC shows including *Top of the Pops* and *Jim'll Fix It*.

Backing up a bit, in 1981, Sutcliffe's trial for multiple murders was held at The Central Criminal Court 'The Old Bailey' (named after the street upon which it stands) in London. Before the proceedings started it was said that Sutcliffe's lawyers asked for a charge of manslaughter with diminished responsibility, and seven charges of attempted murder, thus there should be no trial. This plea was put forward after three psychiatrists had diagnosed him with paranoid schizophrenia. Indeed, the prosecution team accepted that and had every intention of accepting the much lesser plea, but Judge Sir Leslie Boreham was having none of it. He demanded a reason from the prosecution team – and it had to be a damned good one.

You might now be asking yourself how come three so-called leading forensic psychiatrists diagnosed Sutcliffe as suffering from schizophrenia when he was pretty much as sane as the sitting judge? How could three highly-paid shrinks at the taxpayers' expense combine all of their medical intellect to concur in such a monumental diagnostic clusterfuck? Nonetheless, the trial was one of the biggest at the time and covered in the media worldwide, with everyone finding it difficult to understand the warped mindset of a man who claimed God told him to stalk and kill with the voices of the Holy Order speaking in his mind. In fact, the archetypal homicidal sexual psychopath was pulling the wool over everyone's eyes; going on to prove to be one of the most controversial patients at Broadmoor as well as in the entire British prison system. With that said, Sutcliffe was found guilty and in 1981, sentenced to twenty concurrent life sentences (his whole life order given in 2010).

Initially, while using his mother's maiden name 'Coonan', he was sent to HMP Parkhurst just north of Newport on the Isle of Wight. Having struck up brief conversation with an ex-prison officer, I am told that Sutcliffe provided a game of spot the normal inmate; so-called due to him, upon hearing the heavy boots of prison officers approaching his cell, took to wailing and moving backwards and forwards on his bed. It was said by this ex-officer on many occasions his colleagues would remove their boots and approach silently catching Sutcliffe behaving normally. You could only imagine the sense of humour a prison officer possesses, dark with a touch of humility thrown in with a few profanities, the tea break would have been an eventful one. It was said by the ex-officer that Sutcliffe's weird behaviour became more exaggerated as time went on, as did more attempts to catch him out.

It was during his stay on the Isle of Wight that, on 10 January 1983, prisoner James Costello attacked Sutcliffe as he was getting water in a plastic bowl. Costello had with him a coffee jar he'd broken and manufactured to become jagged which he hid inside his prison jacket. Costello attempted to smash the jagged edge of the jar into the left side of Sutcliffe's face. In the ensuing scuffle, Sutcliffe managed to push Costello away before prison officers became involved - while taking their time about it. It was claimed by the former prison officer: 'No man rushed for him (Sutcliffe) when he was in danger'. For his part, Costello was serving time for firearm possession and had received a ten-year sentence and he was also awaiting transfer to Broadmoor hospital being diagnosed as mentally ill. Costello originally from Glasgow had previous form along with twenty-eight previous visits to the courts from 1963 up to 1982. The scars on Sutcliffe's face many would say were well-deserved.

Now here comes the rub because Sutcliffe's behaviour in Broadmoor was almost exemplary. He more-or-less kept himself to himself, his days were used in the pursuit of chasing monsters around TV screens on computer game consoles and reading, then sending letters to equally 'fans'. So let's backtrack to this killer's mental behaviour before his trial, and here is what Christopher Berry-Dee – who has interviewed several 'genuine' paranoid schizophrenic serial killers and has a large collection of their correspondence says. Christopher also corresponded with Sutcliffe, and here is what Chris says:

> 'Prior to his trial starting 5 May 1981, 35-year-old Sutcliffe presented as having most of the symptoms common in paranoid schizophrenics – which according to the Mayo Clinic, in short are: (1) Delusions – false beliefs not based on reality. (2) Hallucinations – usually involving seeing or hearing things that do not exist. (3) Disorganized thinking inferred from disorganized speech. (4) Extremely disorganized or abnormal motor behaviour. (5) Negative symptoms et al.
>
> 'In men schizophrenia symptoms typically start in the early to mid-20s, yet at *no time* prior to 1981, now aged 35, aside from his rapes and murders, he'd presented *not one* of those symptoms; not to his employers, his wife Sonia, her family, his own family nor to any of his workmates and

friends. Then, suddenly upon his arrest these symptoms magically appear. Indeed, the only basis that the three defence psychiatrists based their assessment that he was a paranoid schizophrenic was his fabricated story about hearing the word of God telling him to kill prostitutes. But as we all know Sutcliffe murdered non-working girls too.

'I have interviewed many serial killers who have used this faked 'mentally unfit to stand' their trial defence, amongst them being: (1) Kenneth Bianchi – who claimed that he was a multiple personality. (2) Harvey 'The Hammer' Louis Carignan – who claimed an almost identical defence to Sutcliffe's. (3) Arthur John Shawcross – who claimed a similar defence as Sutcliffe's. Jeffrey Dahmer tried it on in a different way and failed. This is a defence that rarely works, fortunately the judge at Sutcliffe's trial saw through this 'scam' and ruled that Sutcliffe was sane enough to stand in the dock.

'Post-trial there was no appeal; one that might have argued that the judge – him not being a medical professional – had erred, most especially as both defence and prosecution were happy to go along with this phony paranoid schizophrenia yarn…because that was all it was.

More to the point, as soon as Sutcliffe found himself in a mainstream prison all of his self-alleged symptoms vanished like a fart in the wind with him merely faking them when prisoner officers approached his cell – again, a trick that Kenneth Bianchi used…the hiding under the bed trick.

'Around this time, being offered a bed in Broadmoor was much easier than finding a bed in a Butlins holiday camp. Here, in a secure (well as we have seen more-or-less a 'semi-secure) facility, Sutcliffe became, as many former have told me, pretty much a 'normal guy'. He was never heavily sedated, and took up water colour painting has a hobby.

'The reader will find many articles online written by 'professionals' who have interviewed Sutcliffe at length and, bar none, they all formed the erroneous opinion that Sutcliffe was a paranoid schizophrenic. However, they seemed to have missed the point that he was a homicidal psychopath, and these characters are they greatest manipulators of all. They can present to those who are not well-educated in dealing with these offenders to suit their own emotional needs. They have an innate way of 'mirroring' the interviewer. I call this putting on a mask of insanity to suit and taking it off again after an interview is finished. It's like an actor playing a part on-stage to please his audience, yet as soon as the curtain falls they revert to the normal self once again.

'Anyway, having fooled the entire system for decades, and with him actually telling the authorities that he was sane, finally the shrinks at Broadmoor threw their hands up realizing that he'd been conning everyone and the kitchen sink for decades. Sutcliffe was shipped out and spent his final years in a 'proper' prison having stuck two fingers up to all and sundry and good 'an proper too.

'My internationally best-selling book *Talking with Serial Killers: Beyond Evil* covers all of the above subject in great depth….exposing shocking stuff when one realizes that quite often the psychiatrists are as mentally unhinged as their patients.

On a few occasions a celebrity visited the hospital for a photo opportunity and some needed fund raising. Frank Bruno, himself not well due to a nervous breakdown and was invited by Jimmy Savile into the hospital. How is it possible a man well known by the public as fragile, nervous along with being sensitive was used like this? A picture of Bruno is online showing him shaking hands with Sutcliffe, and child-molesting Savile in the background with the self-congratulatory smug face, along with the smoked lensed glasses and the fat Cuban cigar in hand. Great photo opportunity but for who – not for one of the most popular boxers of our time only for the two smug close friends as it eventually came out. Frank Bruno later said in a newspaper interview that he was used and regretted it, along with not realizing with whom he was shaking hands with – 'The Yorkshire Ripper' no less! Superintendent Franey should have been sacked all but instantly, but as will soon become apparent with Franey - who staff later recalled was '…always putting it out there' - and Savile both very seedy characters indeed.

This is how manipulative Savile was, the extremely close friendship between Sutcliffe and Saville lasted from the early years up till 2009, so we might enquire as what drew these two monsters together? Was Leeds the area connection or something more macabre? Two of Sutcliffe's victims' bodies were found very close to Savile's Roundhay Park penthouse flat. It was alleged after the death of Savile, impressions were taken of his teeth and used to compare to bite marks on one of the bodies.

This process is called Forensic Odontology – the most famous case being the impressions taken of Ted Bundy's teeth which proved a perfect match to the bite marks on Lisa Levy's buttocks as she was being killed in the Chi Omega sorority house, Tallahassee, January 1978. And it is at this point we must ask, why are police anxious to keep the results of this postmortem dentistry exercise from the public? How is that Sutcliffe knew that Savile used and abused prostitutes – which he mostly certainly did? And, as we will detail in the next chapter, why, in God's name, did the NHS permit sex monster Savile – a sick beast far worse than Jeffrey Epstein could ever have been – to roam free throughout three of the most secure British high security mental hospitals, given a Golden Key to Broadmoor, his caravan onsite, to mix and sex-play with vulnerable patients? A necrophile sex offender, defiler of dead bodies in mortuaries – oh, yes, just about everyone knew who Savile was - and they *all* kept quiet.

With that said, Sutcliffe still faced some abuse from other patients which Broadmoor hospital tried to play down. Sonia, his wife for a number of years and a doting one at that, separated from him in 1989 and filed for divorce which was granted in 1994.

On February 23rd, 1996, while on Henley Ward Sutcliffe alone in his room was again attacked. Paul Wilson a convicted robber diagnosed as mentally ill by the system, heavy set-in stature knocked on Sutcliffe's door and asked could he borrow a video. In an instant Wilson grabbed a set of headphones from the desk in the room and set about trying to strangle Sutcliffe with the cable. Sutcliffe panicked screamed for help, two other patients, one of them known as the 'Stockwell Strangler' Kenneth Erskine, the other Jamie Devitt, a convicted murderer rushed into the room. Wilson was subdued by the two men before staff nurses restrained Wilson, taking him off to a secure unit. Wilson had an intense hatred of murderers and rapists. Why was Wilson placed on a ward where the likes of Sutcliffe and Erskine two serial killers were placed? Was Broadmoor really achieving its goal of rehabilitation and treatment? Nevertheless, he spent time being pushed from one ward to another throughout the hospital with Savile following him around.

On 10 March 1997 Sutcliffe again came under attack, this time from Ian Kay known as 'The Woolworths Killer'. A felt-tip pen was used to thrust into the left eye of Sutcliffe, along with the right eye receiving severe damage. The left eye of Sutcliffe was damaged so severely his vision was lost. It was said a cheer went up from various patients when the word got out, an ex-security officer confirmed this! A former patient explained to me what sort of feeling was felt throughout the hospital:

'The first thing we knew something was going on when the alarms went off on Henley ward. Ok that's now't different but the radio staff called for the Romeos (security) and told to change channels. I knew it was big, maybe twentyish minutes later we were told not to go near the windows. Yep, a ward full of women going to listen to that! We saw the armed response, the ambulance, police all running, by this time window talk had let the whole hospital know what had happened. Ian Kay spent over a year behind the door for that on I.C.U. Cherwell Ward. He never said to me why he done it, I've asked him loads of times, but he never said. Sutcliffe spent months on the Dunstable Ward (hospital wing) and his arse was kissed so badly by management the cunt got everything he wanted! It made it hard for other staff, they hated him.'

 Sutcliffe's weight increased due to the arse licking from management. When he clicked his fingers to get anything, he wanted, the goose fat roast potatoes were allegedly served at Christmas along with Cranberry sauce. He had developed Diabetes, not uncommon inside high security hospitals. Drugs given for certain conditions can, and do, increase the need for sugar. In Broadmoor patients were allowed to shop for items that included biscuits, chocolate, crisps in the shop though sparsely stocked did contain a varied amount of these products. Settling back into the life of TV, computer games, I have been told by former staff, that he was polite and courteous, with the title of 'Toilet and Bathroom Cleaner' now given to this little shit; the most prolific serial killer the UK has ever seen.

The life inside Broadmoor hospital is unlike a mainstream prison for there is more freedom for those who adhere to the rules along with the treatment. Hospital food never changes though. Portion sizes might, yet dry cabbage and broccoli brings back bad memories for many.

Time and time again after every incident an investigation is held by the hospital and Thames Valley Police, court cases are often held resulting in convictions for those who commit the offences. New procedures are put in place, reviews are taken and more items that cause injury are put on the banned list. Numerous ex-staff have said a day never goes by without the threat of violence: 'You are always on your guard you never let it down, you never turn your back even for a split second you are moments away from a good day turning into a very bad day'.

Patrick Sureda – serving time after being diagnosed as paranoid schizophrenic after strangling his mother in 2000 – was having lunch on Saturday afternoon one December . He was seated just along from Sutcliffe in Dorchester Ward – a lower risk area where patients had access to their own rooms with keys. At the time patients had access to metal cutlery, and Sureda, taking his chance, thrust the metal knife he was using lunged towards Sutcliffe's face. Allegedly tomato sauce flew everywhere as the blade made its way to the cheek area of Sutcliffe's face. Salt, pepper along with the vinegar bottle exploded along with Sureda shouting: 'I'll fucking blind your good eye'. Nurses ran towards the dining area along with other members of staff grabbing hold of Sureda forcing him to the floor and restraint techniques were used to detain him along with attending to the injured Sutcliffe. These injuries resulted in Sutcliffe sustaining a deep cut to his right cheek; although no visit to the local Frimley Park hospital was required this time as the cuts and bruises were said to have been minor. Thereafter, Sureda was placed onto a secure unit within Broadmoor keeping him far away from Sutcliffe. Another internal enquiry along with Thames Valley Police attending with charges being brought, more taxpayers' money being used. Procedures now being put in place where the likes of those who detest each other being kept apart and at no time allowed to come across one and other. Lessons learnt, more training extensive security procedures being brought in, along with the realization that not all incidents are the same.

Life then settles back to normal inside Broadmoor if you could call life in Broadmoor 'normal'.

There are questions still asked about Peter Sutcliffe with no answers being given for the reasons why he was held in the high security hospital with clearly no answer forthcoming from the NHS, or from those who run the system of evaluating the mental state of highly dangerous criminals.

At the time, and up until 2002, the hospital was under the Department of Health. I recall looking back at Sutcliffe's trial that psychiatrists were called upon by the defence and they all came to the same conclusion – that he suffered from paranoid schizophrenia thus was not responsible for his crimes.

So, what had changed during the first few years of Sutcliffe's prison sentence to warrant a move to Broadmoor? Fooling prison guards, the authorities, and a bunch of psychiatrists. Former prison officers have told me about that he played the game of 'fool the guard', and it was a case of let's throw away the key, ship him out of prison and into an asylum, then and forget that he exists. Former prisoner officers who have contacted the author, tell the same story. 'Sutcliffe was not given an easy ride by us, but Broadmoor staff bent over backwards for him.'

We all recall that famous quote from the Stephen King movie *The Green Mile*: 'What happens on the mile stays on the mile', well keeping the public far away from what occurs inside the hospital is a requirement by all who work within. Proud staff will always tell you it's an honour to work there, others will tell you it's dangerous and hard. Staff are the engine room technicians which the hospital relies upon. A tight knit community is encouraged by those who wield the purse strings. Do we really want to pick the bones out of an institution that has and still manages to serve? It has been said by many that the hospital has a village-like feeling to it along with a closed-door policy. For his part, Sutcliffe still posed a problem for several Home Secretaries; keeping him in Broadmoor was a way to keep him away from the outside world, the reason because he was pretty much insane – which he never was. Many say Sutcliffe was a role model patient, maybe too much of a role model. Nonetheless, Sutcliffe was a problem from the day of his arrest, while many demanded the death penalty be re-instated, Prison is too good for the likes of him they said. More uproar continued when Sutcliffe obtained the Broadmoor ticket. The good news is that the new hospital is clinical with clean foundations. Many advances in treatment along with sparkling floors, fresh interior walls, electronic door panels. Rooms with secured furniture, CCTV, no bars on windows just the reinforced type that you would expect in a bank, but the thing that never changes is the danger, and at this point, your author and criminologist Christopher Berry-Dee reveals the most shocking reasons how this sadosexual stone-cold more-or-less conned the system.

***

Forensic Psychiatry: where lead balls bounce, elephants fly and fairies reign supreme – by Christopher Berry-Dee.

'I fooled the psychiatrists. Anyone in a right mind can do it'.

Peter Sutcliffe.

The key question in Sutcliffe's trial was his state of mind when he carried out his attacks. Was he mentally ill, suffering from the rare but clearly definable paranoid schizophrenia? Or was he a clear-thinking sadist who was fully aware of what he was doing, had done, and that he knew the difference between right and wrong and that he could control his actions? In short, was he mad – thus not responsible for his crimes – or guilty of committing multiple homicide with pure malice aforethought?

One of the first grave, almost unforgiveable errors ,was that it was Sutcliffe's defence, represented by James Chadwin QC, who maintained that his client was suffering from paranoid schizophrenia. And, of course, is it not the defence's role to attempt to mitigate a client's crimes, get the sentence watered down, if not completely get one off the hook, yes, of course it is!

To help in massaging a mitigation plea, Chadwin hired three eminent forensic psychiatrists: Dr Hugo Milne of Bradford; Dr Malcolm McCulloch of Liverpool, and Dr Terence Kay of Leeds – each of whom interviewed Peter Sutcliffe. But was this killer interviewed by forensic shrinks hired by the prosecution? The short answer is 'NO!' Can the reader smell a rat here?

What these three 'eminent forensic psychiatrists' believed was to prove crucial to Sutcliffe's claim that, since the age of 20, he had been following instructions from God. He had first heard the word of God seemingly coming from a gravestone in Bingley Cemetery, when he worked there as a gravedigger. This 'voice' told him to clean the streets of prostitutes. God had even helped him by preventing the police from capturing him until now. He conceded that he had been planning to do the Lord's work on Olivia Reivers when police – who had obviously turned a deaf ear to the Lord's instructions – finally caught him. But, as these three eminent shrinks already knew, Sutcliffe had not only killed prostitutes – did he not also murder entirely decent God-fearing young women too - damn right he did!

'The Crown Prosecution Service (CPS)' – perhaps we could say in this case 'The Can't Prosecution Service' – led by Attorney General Sir Michael Havers, limply argued that Sutcliffe's story of a divine mission was a lie and that he was a 'clever callous murderer who deliberately set out to create a cock and bull story to avoid conviction for murder.' C'mon guys and gals, as all of my loyal readers of my own books know, let's say it as it is. One doesn't need to be an Attorney General to figure that out, do we?

Firstly, there was the evidence – which the defence shrinks knew all about – of a prison officer at Armley who had overheard Sutcliffe tell his wife Sonia amidst a string of unprintable expletives that he was planning to deceive the doctors about his mental state. 'I might only get ten years in the fuckin' loony bin', he added, 'I fooled the psychiatrists. Anyone in a right mind can do it.' This was backed up by the fact that during his original interrogation by police, 'The Yorkshire Ripper' never once mentioned a divine mission. Yes, the defence psychiatrists knew this too! Had it not occurred to them that Sutcliffe was faking it…I mean they are the so-called experts on the human mind, are they not? The point I am making here was his ability to do so might have been assisted by the fact that he had at least one personal experience of the illness because in 1972 his wife had suffered a nervous breakdown while studying in London. She had talked of being the Second Christ and had claimed pain in her hands from being nailed on a cross. Sutcliffe would tell his shrinks that he felt a hand gripping his heart.

These facts made it hard to present a convincing case that Sutcliffe really was a paranoid schizophrenic with dangerous delusions. Later, at trial, the jury's distrust in the defence's argument was reinforced when Dr McCulloch admitted that he had taken only thirty-minutes with Sutcliffe to reach a diagnosis. One wonders how much his 'diagnosis' cost the British taxpayer; a hefty sum one can bet on that for sure.

My *Sunday Times* and international bestseller, *Talking with Psychopaths and Savages: A journey into the evil mind*, gives many examples of how psychiatrists are paid big money to mitigate a criminal's crimes when they know otherwise or morally should know better. Many years ago, my paper: *Do psychiatrists have a place in court?* Written on this subject for *The Justice of The Peace,* received much acclaim, for this underhand behaviour is, when it comes down to it, attempting to corrupt the criminal justice system.

But the good news is this. Caught with their professional eminent shrinks' pants down and presently between a rock and a hard place, the defence backtracked saying that if they were 'wrong' about the paranoid schizophrenia then there was only one likely explanation and that was the prosecution's claim that Peter Sutcliffe was a sadist, a man who enjoyed killing women. A cold-blooded murderer, evil rather than mad. Stark raving bonkers he was not and I truly believe with all my heart, that all of my readers past and present – indeed most right-minded folk on Planet Earth – unless they are leaning so far left they are about to topple over will agree that in this case the defence psychiatrists were living in a world where lead balls bounce, elephants fly and fairies reign supreme…or can I say, 'full of mitigational bullshit'? Yes, why not! Ah, yes, the lady wearing the grey rinse at the back asks: 'So if Sutcliffe was not mad, why was he given a bed in Broadmoor Hospital; to be parked up in a so-called place for the criminally insane…the off-the-freaking-wall bouncers…those with many slates missing from their roofs…sandwiches missing from their picnics?'

And, of course, you might be asking the same question of me right now. Well, as is my wont in all of my books, and as all of my readers will know, I also go off-the-wall occasionally and invent a sort of script in which I try to bring us *all* back to down to Planet Earth, so let's continue with these invented Q & A sessions during one of my public talks:

C B-D: Yes, my love, and what a great question.
Lady: Thank you Christopher. I'm from our local St. Jude's Church 'Purl One Knit One' circle. A devout Christian, a teacher of Alpha, once a doctor's receptionist and a one-off two-minute visitor to a Jehovah's Witness meeting (round of applause) so how and why, may I ask, did Broadmoor Hospital take Sutcliffe in when the scrawny bearded turd should have been made to break rocks until the end of his days, had his nuts cut off, better still strung up on some gallows?

C B-D: The short, succinct entirely unprofessional answer, hen, is: 'FUCKKKK only knows'. Perhaps as you are a devout Christian you might ask…

Lady: Yes…

CB-D: ask Our Lord the same question as according to The Gospel of St. Peter the Slayer, they were both accomplices in some kinda way…frankly my dear, I ain't got a clue but let's at least give him a Gold Star for conning the entire British judicial system, the Vegan do-gooders wearing flat shoes and green tights, half of the UK's most eminent forensic psychiatrists, a whole buncha legal eagles, and the taxpayer why this worthless asswipe was given the 5-Star treatment at a cost of millions of quid of our hard-earned cash to live in relative luxury while his victims are now rotting in their graves with the sides falling in. Oh, and my sweet lady. Please don't seek accountability. All those responsible for this mega institutional clusterfuck having now being promoted to higher office.

CB-D: Next question please: Yes, sir. The bald, built like a brick shithouse gent with more tattoos than a fairground worker, a Polish roof tiler. Yes, *you* sir with the salivating Pit Bull Terrier straining at its leash.

Gent: Cheers mate. What about Jimmy Savile?

CB-D: Fab-U-Louse question. As author Boris will explain, we will come to Savile right now.

***

Sir James 'Jimmy' Wilson Vincent Savile OBE KCSG – The King of Perverts.

'We [Savile]were close friends for more than 20 years, we used
to pop into the Palace after the London Marathon.'

Former Broadmoor Superintendent Alan Franey 2011.

'I never knew Savile very well.'

Former Broadmoor Superintendent Alan Franey 2012.

Source: Jimmy Savile and the *Entrance to the Rabbit Hole*.

What follows might well put your own head into a spin, testing your own sanity because what follows is enough to blow any decent person's mind. At times it may seem confusing, but please follow me, so let me set the scene…omelette anyone?

We all should remember 'Eggwina' aka the toffee-nosed, highly opinionated Edwina Currie for her infamous lead-balls-bouncing statement being that '…most of the egg production in this country [UK] sadly is now affected with salmonella' and which sparked outrage among farmers and egg producers, no doubt the chickens too, and caused sales of eggs to decline rapidly by 60 percent. Frequently far too mouthy for anyone else's good, she was described as '…a virtually permanent fixture on the nation's television screen banally uttering just about anything', and 'the most outspoken and sexually interested woman of her political generation.'

In September 1986, Eggwina became a Tory Junior Health Minister. Among her comments over the next two years were – despite her not being one iota religious – that 'good Christian people don't get AIDS.' All but sounding like a Trump rant, she added, '…that old people who could not afford their heating bills should wrap up warm in winter' and that northerners die of, 'ignorance and chips.' The egg controversy, which resulted in the slaughter of four million hens, forced her to resign as Parliamentary Under-Secretary of State for Health in December 1988 - but not before what follows happened.

Advisory Note: please sit down now and get a hold of a very stiff drink, maybe some curried eggs because in

1988, a senior civil servant appointed television personality Jimmy Savile to head up a task force to run – *yes run* – Broadmoor Hospital. Despite scores of circulating rumors that Sir Jim was a running amok paedophile, with Eggwina rubber-stamping this decision he was given extraordinary power and a set of keys with complete access to every part of the hospital. He mingled repeatedly with the 800 or so patients, many teenage girls, some severely disturbed and medicated.

What, you may rightly ask in fuck's name was going on here?

Well it all starts about here with a rum crew headed by two principal characters - Franey and Savile - and what follows makes for very disturbing reading indeed.

'Franey had a little secret…a liking for young girls, the younger the better.'

NHS Executive to Government investigators, an allegation Franey denied despite overwhelming evidence to the contrary (Source: David Hencke, *Political Scrapbook*).

Alan Franey had been recommended for a manager's post at Broadmoor by Jimmy Savile, whom he'd met at Leeds General Infirmary (and where Savile was abusing corpses in the mortuary) and they ran charity races together. There is never smoke without fire and with Savile now enjoying unfettered access to Broadmoor Hospital in the 1980's, his running partner – Franey, later a Tory Counciller for Welwyn Hatfield - and with Savile insisting the job be given to his oily friend, staff at Broadmoor would later tell an NHS enquiry about the closeness between the pair, with Franey asking for the Godfather' when he regularly rang Stoke Mandeville Hospital – where the TV presenter was sexually abusing youngsters at the time.

The set of keys given to Savile created the most sinister part of history for Broadmoor and still today continues to throw up questions that need answering, so let's start with who – meaning a total moron - decided it was acceptable to hand a set of keys to someone who is not qualified in *any* medical field, let alone giving a set of hospital keys to any non-professional at all - yes a set of keys given to someone who was not cleared for security in any highly-secure environment. Money and fame brings one all sorts of pleasures including self-satisfaction. Getting a Knighthood for raising money for charity along with working in TV and radio, with Royalty and Parliament along with volunteering this is the darkest, predator, manipulator, and abuser Jimmy Savile.

According to a Government report, it was 1968 when Savile first got his foot in the door or of the UK's highest profile mental facility housing the most dangerous criminals. Savile contacted the then Superintendent Dr. Pat McGrath; a highly respected individual regarded as the person who was changing Broadmoor's image for the better. It still seemed that many of the staff where unchallengeable and the village-like atmosphere was still prevalent. Savile told the press at the time he was 'voluntary assistant entertainments officer'; self-appointed of course, for he was high profile, always in the papers doing some good along with millions listening on the radio and TV to his quavering gurgle. At the time Superintendent Dr Pat McGrath thought it would be a good idea to get Savile involved helping the hospital to brush up its image. Charity would be the cover story Savile would use to exploit many, in fact records show truly little was raised by Savile for Broadmoor Hospital. The odd donation along with selling a few items contributed to not much more than the occasional treat for patients and staff, with the led-up-the garden-path outside world seeing Savile as some sort of Messiah shining a light on the hospital giving it much needed hip, hip hooray publicity. Some staff feeling uneasy from early on suspecting what Savile was up to, attempted to blow the whistle, but yet again the large shagpile carpet was used to brush it under.

Was there some sort of Old Boys' Club system? 'Cover your eyes and ignore', was allegedly said by some patients. One former female patient told the author, '…yes, it's true, Savile said that to me,' with other allegations that staff were given backhanders to keep their mouths shut also voiced frequently.

Savile started on the path of gaining entry then plotted the route; some wards refused to have him as staff members felt uncomfortable with him around them because he was oily and smug. Other wards were more accommodating, allowing him free reign to come and go unannounced. Staff noticed the frequent visits resulting with the excitement from patients and some staff all clearly evident on the faces seen in photographs. A basic accommodation was afforded to Savile within the non-secure area of the hospital; in the grounds with a parking space for his Rolls Royce. The flat he called 'the cell' was small -one bedroom, kitchen and lounge area including a small trampoline dumped in the middle of the sitting room. Here the sex beast was private and away from staff and patients along with prying eyes. It seems that many members of staff were ex-forces; unlike today staff are recruited or trained from all over the UK and procedures unlike the past are now vastly improved. In the late sixties many of the Broadmoor patients wrote fan letters to Savile, so did this prompt Savile to pen a letter to Pat McGrath, although it was later said by Dr Pat McGrath's son, that his father hated Savile.

Savile used to travel around in various Rolls Royce car's ranging from a Silver Cloud Mk 3 to a red Corniche. a white Range Rover towing his caravan was often seen by many. Bizarre that a caravan nicknamed the 'Passion Wagon' that Savile also owned was allowed to be parked onsite at Broadmoor, often cleaned by the patients along with the car he drove...why? Savile's cars were even serviced in the hospital garage, so talk about bending over backwards for the man worth a fortune, yet tight as a fish's ass. The persona Savile projected at the hospital was one of flamboyance that also included unusual methods of introducing himself to female staff members and patients. Some staff allegedly mentioned him touching their breasts, bottoms and hair. A close atmosphere within the hierarchy was noted by many seeming to have some sort of power over those at the top in the hospital; was money or the fame this man held thought as some sort of ego trip by senior staff – undoubtedly ass-licking was the order of the day.

Young women were held at Broadmoor and one incident involved a 14-year-old who tried to tell staff that Savile had sexually abused her in her room. How did Savile worm his way out of that, a former staff member has told the author, 'It wouldn't have surprised me? The man was a vile human being.'

Former staff who contacted me through www.broadmoorsinister.co.uk were convinced power in high places had something to do with it. Male and female patients were kept separate or so they say, others tell a different story along with orgies and staff and patient relationships. During the 80s female patients were required to strip naked to change into nightwear along with taking baths. Creepy Savile had the ideal opportunity to have a peek during these times through the cracks of doors and small window panels on the doors itself; with all this going on people stood back and watched, listened and did nothing, the closed-door policy of staff who closed ranks, making other staff lives' hell who tried to tell those in higher places what was going on. Notwithstanding, Savile's influence on upper management became stronger worming his way through the corridors of power, not just within the hospital but within those who held ministerial Government positions.

During these darkest of times for the hospital, unions became a big part of daily life; threats of strikes by staff who were members of The Prison Officers Union were often consulted on major issues. Savile's meeting with the then minister Edwina Currie at his request looking to expose false overtime claims made by staff. This is the power this man wielded not just inside the hospital; outside he was just as powerful. Having been put onto the hospital's board after the Department of Health suspended the entire management in 1988, just before a critical report was published Savile having been asked for his input at that time. The outcome placed the hospital under temporary control headed by Savile, yes, the celebrity with no known qualifications in anything to do with Mental Health or any other form of health, how was this possible? Savile, overjoyed at his appointment was seen in local newspapers holding the trademark cigar in the air with the grin of the century. The selection of the next management team involved was headed by Savile who had the last say on the selection to sit at the top table. Some suspect the motive was to have more access to the vulnerable areas of the hospital along with access to those who were vulnerable.

Savile and Peter Sutcliffe's relationship goes back a number of years. Turning a blind eye to this, is one member of the top table team still alive as we write and nowhere to be found. The name of this individual keeps cropping up from those who contact me along with 'you will be lucky to find him' – was money involved, backhanders or something more sinister?

Sutcliffe was first visited by Savile in HMP Parkhurst situated on the Isle of Wight. Letters were sent back and forth between the two; coming to light is Savile's mention of Sutcliffe's name during a police interview at the height of the Ripper spree. Savile's Leeds flat was within yards of two victims of the Ripper! No connection was ever made between the Yorkshire Ripper murders or Savile's possible involvement in them. Odd that! A well-known celebrity was making a play for Sutcliffe, why? Photos doing the rounds showing Sutcliffe and Savile in Broadmoor seemingly being cosy towards each other while Sutcliffe always denying Savile was involved in any way with him. Staff asking questions and being ignored by those higher up continued. Savile's caravan within the walls allegedly being visited by female staff members has often been mentioned; was it for a cuppa, or was Savile using the mobile home as a way of abusing those who were too frightened to blow the whistle? Power mad celebrity status, the trappings of wealth, wave money in front of those, they say a pound note talks!

Allegedly six cases of sexual abuse against patients undertaken by Savile were thought to have happened including one female under sixteen years of age. The excuses, various reports would come up with in the early years, are risible. Looking at the numbers of patients Broadmoor was housing, these ranged from 850 down to 380, during 1970 up to 2001 and numbers of staff were approximately 800. It's fairly easy to see how some events went unnoticed. Female wards throughout had access by a secure area, clearly not the case in all of them, various other entrances were available by the outside area unopposed by security systems. Ideal opportunities to gain access unnoticed by staff. 'Savile presented that Marmite-like product effect you either liked him or not, no in-between', one former security staff member told the author. 'Savile played the predator game, if he knew you were weak, he would find the weakness, pray on it and get his own way.' Some staff would take a harder line than others and it seems those who did on their wards saw less of Savile, and if they did, he would be under strict supervision and escorted. Vulnerable patients throughout the hospital of all ages being taken in by the celebrity status, Savile had a way with getting celebrities involved with the hospital. Even royalty would pop along to open a new area of the hospital when required. Nobody was out of reach for Savile to use for his own ego trip from celebrities to the man, woman or child on the street. A set of keys from the hospital always with him even when away, imagine a prison officer taking a set home or the cashier of the Bank of England doing the same. Some have said the reason for this was to keep those guessing whether he was in or out at the time. The caravan was always locked! No person daring to have a peek to see if the monster was about for fear of upsetting him or those who approved of him.

Pan's People, a popular dance act who appeared on Top of the Pops on BBC1 during the late 60s and early 70s appeared on the Broadmoor stage all set up by Savile. Acker Bilk (MBE) the clarinetist and singer were also persuaded to visit the hospital. Well, one might suppose that if you designated yourself the now 'Senior Entertainments Officer' along with 'Senior Patron of the Staff Club' you might as well go for it. Day trips escorted to Bournemouth for those patients and staff along with the kids who behaved themselves. It was said by some staff the day trips were a way of releasing tension from the stressful job they had. Savile rarely popped along on these trips… was it the fear of being noticed by his adoring public a bit too much for Mr Ego! The yearly Broadmoor Fete attracted local interest with many going along from the village and Bracknell. On a few occasions the well-known associated with Savile made an appearance. Birds of disgusting feathers flock together with Paedophile Rolf Harris sitting in a chair with his utensils used to draw and paint children and adults followed by the autograph. It was said on a couple of times that Harris had a Savile escorted guided tour round the wards of Broadmoor. One of these visits it is claimed was during bath time for the ladies. What thrill did they both gain from the guided tour - what was their relationship like?

So now let us wind back to the relationship with Sutcliffe and ask what drew them two together? It certainly was not the love of being behind walls and wire. Rape and necrophilia even inside the walls of the infamous hospital was alleged to have taken place. Tea and cakes often shared by these two individuals having a natter while sharing horrid stories. What hold did Sutcliffe have over Savile; was it the discovery of two body's awfully close to

Savile's flat in Leeds? Savile did mention Sutcliffe's name during a police interview well before these two even met inside the penal system, odd some would say! Why mention Sutcliffe? Extraordinarily little connection was made between the two. Comfy in Broadmoor, why for years was Sutcliffe's life made easy instead of life inside a normal prison? For all the trappings that fame brought Savile it seems that his generosity was negligible but £500.00 did find its way to someone Sutcliffe knew, all being an alleged charity. Extraordinarily little money was raised by Savile for the hospital even though it looks from the outside he was doing so much. Yes, his boasting that at his own expense and against staff wishes he handed out cans of beer to medicated patients…being can of out-of-date beer he found in a hospital skip, no less.

Could some of the money passed into the hands of those higher up as some kind of payment? It was alleged by some of those lower down the pecking order in the hospital that something was not right. Whistleblowing was frowned upon during these times and often resulted in some form of bullying seeing various people leave the hospital. In today's climate it is called 'constructive dismissal' with large compensation pay-outs. Some staff were made of sterner stuff resulting in Savile not having his own way, former staff members had many times tried to inform the hierarchy, what was allegedly going on? Power having the advantage often see those in the spotlight turn up to the hospital opening new wings, what else was going on within the hospital even convincing MPs he was the one to go to if anything needed addressing. So many questions unanswered by the later report into the Savile years at Broadmoor, excuses used such as: it was the sign of the times, Savile was a celebrity with no questions asked. So much was hidden by those above him who were fired by him why? We can spend time going backwards and forwards with this darkest era of Broadmoor at some point Savile had his reign cut from him. Security was tightened after escapes and the leaking of various information from within the hospital. In 2002 the NHS pulled the plugged on Savile along with his access to keys, installing a management system directly accountable to them. Visits became exceedingly rare after that year, along with the so-called fund raising he claimed he had done for the hospital. Staff felt at ease especially the female staff members.

Savile died on 29 October 2011 in Leeds, at his home in Roundhay, having suffered pneumonia previously. Sticking in the throat of many including ex-staff members of the hospital was the undisputable fact that he never faced charges for any of the sickening crimes he committed. Sticking his fingers up to everyone being laid to rest in a satin gold coffin lined with the last cigar he smoked on top. Encased in concreate as a security measure or was it to prevent any form of forensic analysis at Woodlands Cemetery tilted at a 45-degree angle facing the sea. With the elaborate head stone, now removed along with any sign of who is buried there.

A government report into Savile is 148 pages long published June 2014 does not paint a pretty picture for the hospital. It included 14 recommendations for the Department for Health along with the NHS. There is a total of 44 published reports into Savile's years at various hospitals Broadmoor is just the tip of the iceberg.

END NOTE: During the research for this book the author made three FOI requests for times and dates of Savile's visits and stays at Broadmoor. Two FOI requests went to Broadmoor Hospital, one to the NHS, all were ignored. Oddly enough, after writing to the then Health Secretary Matt Hancock, NHS England initially emailed me inferring *wrongly* that Broadmoor Hospital:

West London NHS Trust, does not need to respond to FOI Requests, then tried to bog me down in legal jargon, with this sea change:

> 'Thank you for your communication of 28 May 2021 in respect of your FOI requests to Broadmoor Hospital.

> 'Please accept our apologies for any confusion. We can confirm that NHS England is a Public Authority for the purposes of the FOI ACT and will respond to requests submitted to NHS England. As was indicated in our reply dated 28 May, however, NHS England is unable to respond on behalf of another Public Authority in relation to requests submitted to that Authority. As your communication was chasing responses to requests which you had submitted to Broadmoor Hospital, which falls under a separate Public Authority, NHS England is unable to respond to those requests, which will need to be handled directly by Broadmoor. They will also need to respond to any complaints about the handling of requests submitted to them.'

Communications Team
Office of the Chairs, Chief Executive Officer and Chief Operating Officer.

Five months went past since the first FOI request was made to Broadmoor Hospital: West London Trust, and still, they refused to comply with the FOI Act…well maybe one day when hell freezes over, so we soldier on.

∗∗∗

John Thomas Straffen.

STRAFFEN -Verb:

Punish to cause to suffer for a crime of fault

Punish to give punishment for

Discipline to punish.

Cambridge Dictionary.

Sirens, sirens, sirens were the wailing alerts Broadmoor Hospital used to broadcast at 10am sharp every Monday morning. They were like a two-tone air raid racket, not quite the same as used in London in WWII but enough to sound throughout the counties of Berkshire and Surrey, and it went like this: The first two minutes of two-tone was followed by a two-minute continuous 'All Clear'. Hear these sirens at any other time of the week and one knew that a 'patient' had escaped – a lunatic was on the loose. Schools went into lockdown with parents ordered to collect their children after classes. Police set up roadblocks, cop-copters whirled overhead, search dogs were sent a-sniffing and even the Army might be called in to search for the escapee. And here is the reason why the sirens were initially installed at Broadmoor – John Thomas Straffen.

A lonely figure, blonde hair, his face as white as plaster cast and over 6ft tall, his most outstanding feature are the blank, dead look in his ice-cold eyes. This is not the sort of man one would want to meet in some damp dark alleyway late at night.

Born 27 February 1930, at an Army camp in Bordon, Hampshire; his father a military man, posted to India when John was two, his mum, a housewife (in U.S parlance 'a homemaker'), according to available records, at the time John Straffen's older sister was regarded somewhat cruelly, as a 'mental defective' who died aged 24. The family returned to the UK in 1938 to settle in crowded lodgings in Bath.

As far as his schooling narrative goes there is little evidence, yet we do know that it was not long before staff noted that Straffen was falling behind his peers, added to which he often played truant, stole the possessions from other pupils, thus, he was referred to a local clinic that dealt with children exhibiting behavioural problems. This was young Straffen's first link to crime, thereafter, he started thieving from shops and stole a purse from a local girl; all of which landed him in court where the beaks awarded him a two-year probation order in 1939, with his probation officer saying: 'John does not seem to know the difference between right and wrong.'

Mrs Straffen was undoubtedly a hardworking mother who later admitted that she never showed much love or give much time towards her brood. Then the probation officer insisted that she take her son to see a psychiatrist for a mental assessment; the conclusion of which that Straffen was certified – like his sister – as a mental defective: as in 'a person of marked subnormal intelligence, or mental illness, incompetency, condition or disease and could be a danger to himself or others,' *et al.*

A report written at that time showed that Straffen now aged 10, had the mental age of a six-year-old with an IQ of 56, so he was sent to the specialist school, Sambourne, in Warwickshire. With two years here and no improvement at all, he was moved to Besford Court, a school for slightly older children. Once again, psychiatric reports reveal that there was no improvement and, that young Straffen did not take well to discipline. Furthermore, it has been claimed that he suffered from autism, that he had Asperger's Syndrome, but while 'autism' almost fits genetically with his sister's mental issues, as does 'Asperger's Syndrome', yet there is no history of autism or Asperger's Syndrome in his family history, this does not fit with the fact that in 1951, when Straffen, now aged 21, was examined at a Bristol hospital, and electroencephalograph readings showed that he had, '…suffered wide and severe damage to the cerebral cortex, probably from an attack of encephalitis in India before age six.'

It is here, in India, that I find most probably the start of this lad's and his sister's mental problems. If the reader wishes to follow up on this and the causes of encephalitis, it should be noted that between 2008 and 2014, there were more than 44,000 cases and nearly 6000 deaths from encephalitis in India – particularly in Utta Pradesh and Bihar (the latter where John's father was stationed way back when this problem was all but out-of-control). Indeed, as late as 2016, there was a rise in encephalitis, with over 125 children reported to have died in one hospital in Gorakhpur alone.

Stratton started to stray further from what mental normalcy he did possess. Aged 14 it was reported that he was seen strangling two geese in the grounds of the school. Aged sixteen, his IQ was that of a nine-year-old. In March 1946 he'd returned home in Somerset, and where the authorities took the decision to examine him further; the outcome being that he was placed into a secure unit for a brief period under the Mental Health Act. Straffen then took local, low-paid jobs, and none lasted long with his last work being as an unskilled machinist in a clothing factory. In 1947, a young 13-year-old girl reported to police that Straffen had placed his hands over her mouth and said, 'What would you do if I killed you...I've done it before?' An argument between the girl's father and Straffen ensued then shortly after the row Straffen went to the man's house and strangled six chickens owned by the family. He was soon arrested, admitting what he'd done along with other various thefts and low-level crimes.

Straffen's first spell in a main prison came after he was remanded in custody at HMP Horfield in Bristol. 17 prisoners were hung in this grim place, the last 'topping' on 17 December 1963, when one Russell Pascoe was hanged for murder. The death penalty on the UK was abolished in 1969, although working gallows at HMP Wandsworth were kept in order until 1998, when treason was still defined as a hanging offence along with piracy with violence. Nonetheless, it was during this remand period that a medical officer examined young Straffen concluding, once again, that he was 'feeble-minded'. From Horfield, Straffen was transferred to the first purpose-built facility designed to care for up to six hundred mentally disturbed patients. It is of interest to note that Bristol City Council had purchased the 126-acres of land upon which was built the 'Hortham Idiot Colony' which finally closed its doors in 1991. Straffen seemed to settle in well, so much so it was felt that he could be transferred to another facility in Winchester where there was a hostel that catered for those who were considered - although at some risk to themselves - were allowed day-release. So it may come as no surprise to learn that he was soon in trouble again. At a local shop he pinched a bag of walnuts and a couple of tangerines then left without paying. He was arrested and sent back to Hortham but was soon on his toes leaving the place without permission and caught by police during which he received minor injuries during the scuffle.

It was in 1951 that Straffen was subjected to an electrocephalograph examination at a local hospital; a non-evasive procedure where the patient has electrodes placed along the scalp. The readings showed that he had suffered severe damage to the cerebral cortex from encephalitis. In short, this was probably caused by some virulent virus such as rabies. With that now more-or-less confirmed, the doctors considered it just fine for Straffen to return to his home to live with his mother without any monitoring. Now 21-year-old Straffen could taste freedom at last. He found work in a local market garden, and by this time little by little his mental age improved to an IQ of a 10-year-old with more assessments over longer periods of up to six months required.

Although a loner, the cinema was often frequented by Straffen where, at least, he could try and socialise with others. But it is his visit to the 'flicks' on 15 July 1951 that now comes to our notice. As he ambled past 1 Camden Crescent, Bath, he passed five-year-old Brenda C. Goddard who was picking flowers in the front garden of her foster parents' home. 'Can I show you a better place to pick flowers?', suggested Straffen. Following this, he grabbed her, hurled her over a fence into a copse and strangled her, to merely dust himself off and walk off without a care in the world to the cinema where he watched the 1949 noir/crime film *Shockproof*, starring Patricia Knight and Cornel Wilde – all worth a watch if one is interested in a parole officer bonking a dishy, hard-luck dame who has just spent the past five years in the slammer for killing some hard-luck mug who had fallen for her too. With that promo out of the way, during his later police interview, Straffen claimed that Brenda had fallen and had hit her head on a stone. Brenda is buried in Locksbrook Cemetery, Lower Weston, Bath.

Following the Brenda's murder, initially the cops didn't suspect that Straffen was a violent individual, yet information led them to interview him on

3 August and visiting his employer to ask about his movements. He was cleared.

On 8 August, Straffen again went to a picture house where, outside, he met 9-year-old Cicely Dorothy Batstone, and convinced her to go with him to another cinema, the Odeon at 16 Southgate Street. They hopped onto a bus then alighted at a meadow called Congrove Field – known by locals as 'The Tump'. Here he strangled the little girl with his bare hands. Cicely is also buried in Locksbrook Cemetery – fittingly yet tragically her grave is next to that of Brenda's.

The following morning with the hue and cry raised over Cicely's disappearance, a local police officer's wife mentioned to him that the previous evening she'd noticed a man acting suspiciously in the company of a little girl. The off-duty policeman alerted his sergeant, and the woman took officers to the area where she saw the man and police discovered the body of Cicely.

As in all missing child cases, scores of witnesses started to phone police and one tip came from a former work colleague of Straffen's who now was a bus driver and he the tipster recalled seeing Straffen with a little girl on his bus during the evening of the murder. A couple who were in the meadow had spotted Straffen acting strangely near where the child's body was found, and these descriptions led police to Straffen's home where he was arrested on suspicion of murder. Being simple-minded to the enth degree, Straffen 'coughed' immediately and confessed the murder of Cicely and Brenda – the latter he referred to as 'the other girl'. He was remanded after a two-day hearing, with his defence solicitor putting forward the mental age of their client in their arguments and mitigation – the date was 31 August 1951.

Straffen's trial was set for 17th October 1951, Mr Justice Oliver – Peter Raymond Oliver, Lord Baron Oliver of Aylmerton (1921-2007) –

presided over proceedings at Taunton Assizes which lasted one day with Dr Peter Parkes the medical officer at Horfield reading out Straffen's medical and psychiatric history - concluding correctly that the young man in the dock was unfit to enter a plea. And, correctly, the judge said: 'We do not try people that are insane'; the jury being directed to return a verdict of insanity. One might say that Straffen got off lightly for he could have been sentenced to death by hanging, but was the judge correct in saying that the young double killer was insane?

The standard legal test for insanity is the M'Naughton rule. It is used in many forms, the substance of which is almost always the same in many countries including the U.S. The M'Naghten rule wording is specific.

> '...that every man is to be presumed sane, and...that to establish a defence on the ground of insanity, it must be clearly proved that, at the time of committing the act, the party accused was labouring under such a defect of reason, from disease of the mind, as not to know the nature and quality of the act he was doing; or if he did know it, that he did not know what he was doing was wrong.'

It was firmly established that young Straffen did have a 'disease of the mind' – it having been brought about by contracting encephalitis in India. It is also correct to say that the 21-year-old did have an IQ of a 10-year-old and was feeble-minded, aka, a form of high-grade mental deficiency, yet taken *together* does a low IQ, a disease of the mind and feeble-mindedness constitute insanity in Straffen's case? In other words, did he understand that when he committed murder most foul that it was wrong?

Feeble-minded may be defined as:

'[P]persons who may be capable of earning a living under favourable circumstances, but are incapable from mental defect, existing from birth or from an early age, of: (1) of competing on equal terms with their normal fellows or: (2) of managing themselves and their affairs with ordinary prudence.'

Straffen's mental narrative fits perfectly here, but is it not somewhat remarkable that not one of the psychiatrists who had previously examined him as far back as aged 10 ever thought about him being insane. Besides, there are millions of feeble-minded people round the world, and they don't commit double child homicide, do they? Of course, Straffen knew that by abducting and killing those little girls he was breaking the law – that he had a feeble-mind should have been no legal defence, whatsoever. He was a sexual psychopath thru-and-thru, and that is not any mitigation whatsoever.

As is so often in cases such as this, Straffen was given a bed at Broadmoor Hospital. It was determined that he would serve a natural life tariff only to be released wearing a pine box. For his part, for a young man who according to doctors did not know what planet he was residing on, John Thomas Straffen had other ideas and was as equally determined to escape.

'Let him have it, Chris'.

Derek Bentley to Christopher Craig.

At this point in John Straffen's narrative, we should pause to look at another case; that of Derek Bentley who, aged nineteen, with a mental age of 10 years, 4 months, and an IQ of 66 (as was Straffen's), was found guilty of murder and hanged in 1953. Derek, and accomplice 16-year-old Christopher Craig were attempting a burglary at a warehouse in Croydon. The police were called. On the flat rooftop Craig fired a revolver and shot PC Miles through the forehead. As tragic is murder of anyone, the police realised that they could not bring a hanging case against Craig because of his age. They would seek retribution and put a rope around Bentley's neck instead.

Christopher Berry-Dee's book *Dad, Help Me Please* – the title coming the lad's last words to his father before execution – is based on Top Secret Section 5 (1) 'Extended Closure' documents which the Home Office had decided should never be made public for at least a 100-years. Smell a rat? These documents proved the police fit-up; that Derek had no idea that Craig was carrying a firearm that fatal night and that when he shouted 'Let him have it Chris', Derek was already under arrest and was begging Craig to give up the gun.

On a lighter note, when police realised that the Lord Chancellor's Office had inadvertently released photocopies of this Section 5 (1) file, which included police drawings, statements etc, to Christopher, within a week they came hammering on his country cottage door, demanding that he hand them back. 'But I paid £18.00 for them, look here's the receipt,' he explained tongue-in-cheek, and Chris says it went something like this:

Police: Look, Mr. Berry Dee, sir, the Lord Chancellor's Office says you can't have them, so hand them over...please, Sir!

C B-D: But they sold them to me… ummm, do you have a search warrant?

Police: No, sir. Mr. Berry-Dee can we call you Christopher…we are only doing what we've been told to do…please?

C B-D: Nah! As I paid for them all legally, I have made dozens of copies. One set has gone to Frazer Ashford at Crystal Vision in Croydon. Another to the *Daily Mail*, and I'm doing a TV expose next week…my publishers W.H Allen are doing my book. Bye, bye.

The feeble-minded Bentley was convicted as a party to the crime, by the English law principle of common purpose, aka 'joint enterprise', as the burglary had been committed in mutual understanding. Nonetheless, the trial was hugely controversial at the time, but the then Home Secretary refused to intervene in the death sentence passed down by the trial judge, the no-nonsense Lord Chief Justice Goddard.

Published in 1990 by W.H. Allen, *Dad Help Me Please* became a bestseller, to become the No. 1 *Readers' Digest Yearbook* lead title, then the 1991 motion picture *Let Him Have It* starring Christopher Eccleston. The book was reviewed by a later Home Secretary, and, on 29 July 1993, Derek was granted a Royal Pardon. *Dad Help Me Please* was Christopher's first book, and it shows just how crooked some police can be, because while a simple-minded loving son devoted to his pets, Derek had not hurt even a fly in his 19-years, yet circa the same time this double child killer, John Straffen, was given a comfy bed in Broadmoor Hospital, a great diet, free health care and allowed to wander around the lush gardens of his own free will. Where is the fucking justice in that?

*

At the time Straffen was 'given a bed' at Broadmoor, only three-metre-high walls with no razor wire or exterior floodlighting existed. Work details were and have always been part of life within Broadmoor; gardening duty, painting inside and outbuildings, and it was during one of these outside jobs, on 29 April 1952, passing a shed at about 2.45 p.m., in a west-facing area, Straffen leapt up onto the shed roof, scaled the three-meter wall to land in a heap outside of the perimeter. He threw off his overalls and ran towards Crowthorne's high street, then sprinted in the direction of Finchampstead, climbing fences, darting across roads to make his way through a farmer's field, ending up in the village of Farley Hill, some 6.5 miles from the hospital. This distance would have taken him about 3 hours 30 minutes for Straffen, and it was during this period that some of the hospital staff noticed that he was missing. A massive manhunt ensued with Thames Valley police swarming the locality while staff frantically went looking for their escapee in the hospital grounds.

After he'd been on his toes for around four hours, police finally caught him, placing in handcuffs following a violent struggle resulting in Straffen getting a black eye. Under questioning at Wokingham Police Station, he was asked if he had committed any crimes while on the run. He replied, 'I did not kill her.' 'Kill who?' asked an officer. 'I did not kill the girl on the bicycle,' Straffen replied nonchalantly. The police were perplexed, then knowing how dangerous this double child killer was they began a search. 24-hours later, Linda Bowyer was found dead in a ditch. She had been strangled.

Straffen was charged with the murder of Linda and sent to HMP Brixton. Opened in 1820, during the early years if featured a treadmill set into two cast iron wheels that drove a shaft used to mill corn or to pump water for the prison. This is what 'hard labour' was all about said a trial judge – and it's a damned pity it's not used today. Can one imagine what two years treading that wheel would do for prisoners – six men confined in a box on steps that continuously moved when one walked? I betcha that would lower the recidivism rate instead of all the pampering and Human Rights malarky these lowlifes enjoy today.

The trial of Straffen was set for 21 July 1952, with him pleading 'Not Guilty, M'lud' – his defence team took option of leaving the question of insanity to be decided by a jury. The prosecution, led by Sir Reginald Manningham-Buller (1905-1943), was the 1st Viscount of Dilhorne, also known as 'Lord Dilhorne, being Solicitor General 1951 through 1954. He served as Lord Chancellor until 1964. A formidable advocate, Straffen's defence team was somewhat out of their league.

A jury was sworn in, then during the evening one of them recalled that a fellow juror in a nightclub had claimed that someone else was guilty of Linda's murder. Word got back to His Honour Mr Justice Cassels, who, irate, dismissed the jury and empanelled a fresh one. At one point, the disgraced juror was forced to apologise, with the judge calling him 'wicked and evil'. Trying their best to get their 'client' off of the hook, Straffen's barrister called doctors, psychiatrists, even former prison medical officers, with one of them recalling Straffen saying: 'Murder is wrong because it is one of the Ten Commandments'.

The jury didn't buy any of it. After 55-minutes they reached a guilty verdict. The judge donned the black cap and spoke the dread words:

'The sentence of this Court is that you will be taken from here to the place whence you came, and these be kept in close confinement until the date of your execution. And, upon that day you be taken to the place of execution and there hanged by the neck until you are dead. May God have mercy on your soul. Take him down!'

As side notes, of interest the words 'God have mercy on your soul' is believed to have come from the Israeli Beth Din Courts, as in giving authority to God who was thought to be the author of all law. Most probably coming from Deuteronomy 16:18: stating: 'Judges and officers shall make Thee in all thy gates, which the Lord they Giveth thee, tribe by tribe and they shall judge the people with righteous judgment.'

Of further interest is that British judges always used to break the nibs of their pens after pronouncing the death sentence. Indian judges have been following the same custom of breaking their pens after the death sentence was handed down since the British Raj. Here are several of the reasons:

1: the practice is symbolic of the belief that a pen used to take a life away a person's life should not be used ever again for other purposes. In other words, the pen has 'tasted blood', thus it needs to be snapped so that it doesn't take another life.

2: after the death is sentence is passed down, the judge has no power to review or revoke his order. Thus, once it has been awarded, the judge's signature inked, the nip is also broken, symbolic of the fact that the sentencer cannot cancel or rewrite the judgment if he/she has a change of heart or mind.

3: some are also of the belief that judges simply do away with the 'tainted' pen (having ordered the death of a person) as a way of distancing him or herself from the judgment and some guilt of the same.

There has been one recorded exception, that of Lord Chief Justice William Edgar Rayner, Baron Goddard after he'd sentenced Derek Bentley to death. His no- nonsense reputation was reflected in a number of nicknames that he acquired, including: 'The Tiger', 'Justice-in-a-Jiffy', and from Winston Churchill, 'Lord God-damn'. He was considered one of the last 'hanging judges. He did not break his pen, later telling a fellow judge 'I hope to use the same pen again and again'. One judge who most certainly snapped his pen was Sir Justice Thomas Townsend Bucknill, a fellow freemason of the accused murderer, Frederick Henry Seddon. On 14 March 1912, Sir Thomas found it almost impossible to pass sentence of death without breaking into tears, urging Seddon to make peace with his Maker.'

There, we learn a little bit more every day, do we not, and why not I say? 'Nonetheless, Straffen immediately appealed on the grounds of his mental illness; added to which, he sought a legal loophole in that he was not cautioned when he admitted the two Bath homicides. The appeals were dismissed and leave to appeal to the House of Lords refused, but oh, dear, had that been the end of the matter and the end of Straffen at the end of a hempen rope, one would have that nosy Home Secretary, David Maxwell Fyfe, 1st Earl of Kilmuir and former prosecutor at the Nuremburg Trials, also one of the key people who drafted the European Convention on Human Rights, recommended to the Queen that Straffen be reprieved.

This appeal was successful. In November 1952, Straffen was moved to HMP Wandsworth with Rampton Hospital for the criminally insane strenuously denied by the pen-pushing Home Office him a bed there. In 1956, Straffen was moved, this time to more familiar landings, screws, and bars – HMP Horfield, Bristol. This caused an uproar with 12,000 local residents signing a petition demanding that he moved far, far away. HMP Cardiff was next to greet Straffen. He stayed there until 1960, then he was shifted back again to HMP Horfield. I mean one could not this up if one tried – and I have tried VERY HARD not to – because in 1966 he was relocated to HMP Parkhurst on the Isle-of-Wight. 'What the fuckkk was this all about?' you might rightly ask. 'All our taxpayers' money bouncing this triple child killer around the penal system like a rubber ball.' In 1968, Straffen was moved again, this time to HMP Durham, with many prison officers saying that he was 'aloof and hostile towards them on many occasions.'

On 19 November 20017, Straffen died having served 55-years' of incarceration. At that time, he was the UK's longest serving prisoner…oops we must be more politically correct these days. 'Client' is more PC in current times. Yet, there is an endnote here: soon after his escape from Broadmoor it came to light that a witness saw a 'tramp' with Linda Bowyer around the time that she was taken. Apparently, this timing did not match with the distance Straffen had travelled that day and was finally detained hiding behind the Bramshill Hunt public house. The witness said:

> I saw Straffen in Farley Hill at 6 p.m... Linda Bowyer was
> some way off. He [Straffen] would not have had time to get to
> the girl…the tramp came out of nowhere. He came out of the

copse where Linda was found. That was about 5.55 p.m. Was
the wrong man convicted?'

Criminal history is littered with cretinous people who make false claims to get
themselves into the media limelight, so I will leave it at that. The good news
is that Broadmoor's patient escape sirens were installed in 1952 to be
decommissioned in 2019.

***

Frank Samuel Mitchell.

> 'Lizzie Borden took an Axe.
> And gave her mother forty whacks.
> When she saw what she had done
> She gave her father forty-one'.

'The Mad Axeman' will go down in the grim annals of British criminal
history as a Viking fan and their favourite too – the axe, their go-to tool for
just about every job from chopping down trees to making boats to invade
Britain; go a pillaging and raping and burning, and for a damn good case of

hacking and whacking we need look no further than Miss Lizzie Borden (1860-1927). As all you criminology-minded folk know, straightlaced Lizzie was acquitted of killing Ma Abby and Pa Andrew, although she was as guilty as sin. And here is a thing. The murder house on 230 Second Street, Fall River, Massachusetts, still stands pretty much the same (lick of paint or two) and is now a museum and a B&B. Hey, guys and gals, you can even book Ma's old bedroom – if you don't mind a few strange loud thumps in the night.

Frank Mitchell, one of seven siblings, was born in Limehouse, East London, in 1929; his father a fishmonger, life was a drudge, hobbies few and far between. I love trivia, don't you, and the name 'Limehouse' relates to the local kilns - more precisely lime oasts - by the Thames, all of which were operated by the largest potteries serving shipping in the London Docks. The name is 'Old English' *līm-āst* 'lime oast'. The earliest reference to *Les Lymhostes*, in 1356. But here is something I bet you didn't know but soon will: the name 'Limehouse' is sometimes mistakenly thought to be derived from the nickname for the seamen who disembarked there; they who had earned the name 'Lime-juicers' or 'Limeys' after the obligatory ration of lime juice the Royal Navy gave their sailors to ward off scurvy…okay, okay, enough already so back to Frank.

From a very early age Frank was a problem for the authorities. Cycle thefts, slapping other kids around and truanting, aged nine he was in Juvenile Court for nicking a bike from another child. He was placed on probation. Good-looking, with sharp features and size thirteen feet, his hands the size of small shovels, this was a youth everyone started to fear. He was placed in Borstal aged 17, to cause no end of trouble: rioting; setting bedding ablaze and beating the living daylights out of any other lad who crossed him. One

Borstal officer received a beating from Mitchell during a riot in Rochester. Late night shop break-ins were his next target, home burglaries, managing to get a young girl pregnant, more Borstal time,' so we can certainly say that young 'Man Mountain Mitchell' had no intentions of becoming a priest.

At one time he was charged with attempted murder following an attack on another inmate. 'He grassed on me', said Mitchell in his defence. During the incident, an officer had his cheeks slashed. Nonetheless, Mitchell received ten whacks with the birch, then, while in 1952, serving time at HMP Wandsworth, he fell in with the Kray Twins.

With Mitchell becoming more unpredictable by the month and now diagnosed as a mental defective, he was sent to Rampton psychiatric hospital, from whence two years later he escaped with another patient. While on the run, he attacked a man with an iron bar and stole his victim's clothes and money. Soon recaptured and during his arrest he attacked two police officers with a meat cleaver. This was a man who could lift up the heavy end of a grand piano or with one hand hoist any man right off of his feet.

'There is no prison that can hold me. I am impossible to keep locked up. You will not hold me!'

Frank Mitchell.

Furious with the escape from Rampton, the authorities sent him to yes, you've guessed correctly, Broadmoor. 1957 finds him 'licking windows because they taste of bananas' and taking an avid interest in the pink windmills that he thought 'growed' in the vast gardens. His other interest was bouncing other patients and some staff off of walls; telling vivid stories to those wide-eyed patients of even less intelligence than he about how he managed to evade capture while on his toes, and boasting that no prison could keep him locked up, to which the staff took little notice.

With the hospital's doctors believing that Our Frank was a total fruit cake and had completely lost the proverbial plot and all of his marbles too, it transpires that he was not as stupid as they had concluded. There is often the misconception that if one is totally backward at school – which he was, that's when he actually did go to school – one can be extremely cunning and streetwise. This author asks: what use would have been algebra to Frank, even *some* of the Alphabet, when embarking on a career as a burglar, thug and downright public nuisance? Thus, it was on a bright sunny day when 'Window Licking Frank' peered spotted that the perimeter wall was, let's say scalable. He would do a bunk. Taking his chance, Frank pole-vaulted the wall then merrily hopped and skipped down the hill towards Crowthorne, to make his way along Old Wokingham Road, admiring the views and whistling the tune *Watch with Mother*. If the reader would like to hear this tune go look on YouTube – the author did ☺.

Passing Heathland's Farm, Honey Hill, he jumped into a field of strawberries, ate a few handfuls of the juicy fruit, laid down looked up at the blue skies fluffy clouds and took a well-earned rest with even more trivia, because you can find the farm on Google Maps. But soon Frank was on his feet; this lumbering giant passed over railway lines before strolling into Wokingham. Sticking out like a sore thumb, with several police forces trying to track him down, he knocked on someone's door. It was opened by a middle-aged man. Frank, now holding an axe he had stolen from the garden shed, forced his way in and made the homeowner to sit with his wife on a settee. 'Tea and cakes, please,' he told them, 'I'm staying for a couple of days.'

Frank's initial intention had been to make a telephone call to some cronies in London so they could come and get him – but he had forgotten the number. Three days passed when police finally located him. Now fed up holding the couple hostage, he made a run for it still holding the axe. Police later explained that 'Mitchell put up a fight with six officers and we used force to apprehend him.' Finally, Broadmoor's 'All-Clear' siren shrieked pout throughout the area. Locals could now sigh collective breaths of relief.

Mitchell's friendship with the Kray Twins had started earlier with Ronnie Kray paying for Mitchell's solicitor on the attempted murder charge. The Krays also paid for bespoke suits for Frank to wear. And to prove to the authorities that the twins didn't take kindly to the authorities giving Frank a tough time, a plan was hatched to engineer his breakout. However, as can be seen, Frank was quite capable of escaping from almost any place – his problem, one of not some insignificance, being that whilst on the run hiding was not his professional forte.

In 1962, Frank was behind grey-walled HMP Dartmoor in Princetown aka 'The prison that broke both the heart and the soul'. Pretty much permanently shrouded in mist, it was opened in 1809 and designed by Daniel Asher Alexander (1768-1846). An engineer as well as a surveyor to the London Dock Company, this handsome fellow also is known for his Trinity House lighthouse designs being their surveyor too. So, if you are ever in the near vicinity of either the South Stack or Farne Island lighthouses, you can totally and unquestionably amaze your wife and bored-to-fuck kids by saying: 'Hey, wow. Look over there. That was designed by Daniel Asher Alexander (1768 – 1846). And *you won't believe this,* but he designed Dartmoor Prison too!'

Frank Mitchell behaved himself. He became a trustee – a red band - with errands including digging trenches or doing jobs for the prison governor. On several occasions he took a taxi into Okehampton to buy odds and ends, one being a budgerigar. He even was allowed to visit the local pubs for a beer or two. He had a mistress for a while, making love in a local barn. Yes, the Governor trusted Our Frank so much so that he promised 'The Birdman of Dartmoor' that he would highlight his case so that the Parole Board would take this excellent behaviour into account. Nevertheless, four years dragged by with him becoming 'Frank the Impatient', so he contacted Ronnie Kray and between them they hatched an escape plan. 'The Birdman of Dartmoor' had done enough 'bird' (prison parlance for doing time) and the date was set for 12 December 1966, when Ronnie, wearing a disguise, visited Mitchell, saying: 'If nothing else it would stick two fingers up to the law.' So on this auspicious day, Frank was on a work party out on the moors and he asked the sole prison officer if he could feed some ponies nearby. With no objection, Mitchell, the Governor's favourite, was allowed to wander off and make his way to a car parked a short distance away. The driver was Albert Donoghue 'Mad' Teddy Smith and with him was Billy Exley. The car sped off. The prison officer was unaware until sometime later, when the prison van turned up to collect the prisoners and the head count was one short. Reminiscent of a scene from the TV sitcom *Porridge*, the officers scratched their heads and shrugged their shoulders saying: 'Well, the ponies must have run off with him,' and staggeringly it took five hours before the alarm was raised which by this time Frank was back in 'The Smoke' – London of course – and holed up in a Barking flat. He would stay here for the next twelve days.

Two hundred police, one hundred Royal Marines Commandos from CTC RM, a RAF helicopter and a dog were now out on the soaking wet moors searching for who the newspapers called 'Britain's Most Dangerous Man'. Teddy Smith penned a letter to the press on Mitchell's behalf, pleading for a release date – somewhat ironical as Frank had already released himself. *The Times*, the *Daily Mirror* along with the green-wellie brigade's *Horse and Hounds* – because somehow ponies were involved in the escape – with locals being asked to keep a lookout for giant of a man riding a pony, Labour Home Secretary Roy Jenkins issued a blunt statement: 'We are *not* willing to negotiate with an escaped felon and would not review it till he is back behind bars.'

Although breaking huge rocks in the quarry had always been part of Dartmoor Prison's punishment regime, Frank now found himself between an even larger rock and an even harder place. Unable to venture out or move around as he had been doing almost at will while banged up, he became violent towards his hosts. The Kray Twins refused to visit him for fear of giving the game away and becoming implicated with loose cannon Frank Mitchell. To try and placate him, women were allowed to visit him, one being bottle-blonde Liza Prescott who worked in a nightclub owned by the Krays, but then Frank took a shine to a brunette which caused even more problems than previously. Now with Christmas coming up fast, he demanded to see his family. The Krays came hatched a solution, Frank would have to be killed!

At 8.30 p.m. Christmas Eve 1966, Mitchell was taken by Donoghue to a waiting van with Frank assuming that he was being taken out of London to a safer address. Lying in wait was Freddie Foreman and Alfie Gerrard, both carrying handguns. As the engine was started, they opened fire on Mitchell - it is said 12 shots in all, before Frank died.

If we look back on Mitchell's life, for all of his problems and troubles the killing of Frank might seem an unnecessary act, for letting him go free would have been the better outcome for he was no grass. 'But business is business' the Krays would later emphatically say. For the Twins this was a crisis: if he escaped he could wreck 'The Firm' by implicating them all.

Foreman has claimed that chicken wire was used to wrap up Frank's bullet-ridden weighted corpse then dumped into the sea to sleep with the fishes. Donoghue became a Crown witness to grass up Reggie Kray which resulted in a five -year prison term for conspiring to help someone escape from prison. John Dickenson got eighteen-months for harbouring a fugitive. Foreman was in arrested in 2000 after confessing on television to the shooting, but under the 'Double Jeopardy Rule' the CPS dropped the case.

The Krays always maintained that Mitchell was smuggled out of the country and set up with a new identity abroad while always refusing to specify where. Ronnie had it that the only reason they aided Frank's escape was to raise moral in 'The Firm' as the Richardson gang was gaining dominance. Springing Frank Mitchell was merely a means to an end, with the Krays knowing all too well that Frank would be a liability in any event, so the yarn about Mitchell being giving a new identity and set up at significant risk to The Firm overseas is all hogwash.

Officially today, The Home Office confirms that Frank Mitchell is still on the run from Dartmoor. Dickenson tells a different story to that of Foreman's; that Foreman and others took Frank's body out into the countryside where it was cut up and burned. He also claimed that Foreman had described Mitchell's brain as tiny, and that when they removed his heart there were three bullets lodged inside it.

For all that Frank Mitchell had done during his thirty-seven years, can we ask, did he deserve such a terrible ending? 'The Mad Axeman' only obtained this nickname because of the Wokingham hostage taking when by all accounts he treated his captors with some respect if one can call it that? And after all it was 1966 when England won the World Cup in which most of the team played for West Ham United. The Kray Twins thought of themselves as 'untouchables' in running much of London's seedy, crime-ridden underworld. The Home Office was furious that 'The Mad Axeman' was allowed to wander off of from prison of his own cocky freewill, but at least the sirens at Broadmoor worked.

'Andrew Borden now is dead,
Lizzie hit him on the head.
Up in Heaven he will sing,
On the gallows she will swing.'

***

Graham Frederick Young.

'Bureaucracy…the giant power wielded by intellectual pygmies.'
French novelist and playwright Honoré de Balzac (1799-1850) *Les Employés*,
1838.

N.B. The author has devoted a much more comprehensive chapter to our next Broadmoor resident as this highlights some of the serious bungles that the hospital's psychiatrists, nursing staff, the Home Office, a complete fool of a Home Secretary, and numerous mental health boards and Tribunals in British criminal history have ever clocked up. Rank incompetence is rife throughout, yet not one single person was held accountable, so cuppa tea anyone – well think again if your host was Graham Young aka 'The Teacup Poisoner' and forgive us authors if this chapter leaves an acrid taste in your mouth, let's start at the beginning…no sugar please!

Fascinated by poisons, a devotee of Nazism and black magic, Graham Young remains an enigma. Born 7 September 1947, at Willesden Maternity Hospital, Honeypot Lane in Neasden, Middlesex, his mother Molly (elsewhere called Bessie or Margaret depending on the source) had contracted pleurisy during pregnancy and died of tuberculosis when he was three months old.

Following Molly's death, Graham's father Fred, a machine setter, sent his 8-year-old daughter Winifred to live with her grandmother in nearby Links Road while Graham was raised by Fred's sister Winnie Jouvenat and her husband Jack at 768 North Circular Road, a comfortable, modern terraced house with a garden. The lad was close to the Jouvenats, whom he called 'Aunty Panty' and 'Daddy Jack' and showed affection to their daughter Sandra. A chubby, freckle-faced little boy, he was fondly nicknamed 'Pudding'.

Fred Young remarried on 1 April 1950. His second wife – also called Molly –was an attractive, younger woman who played the accordion at a local pub. The family was soon reunited. Fred, Molly and Winifred joined Graham at North Circular Road, while the Jouvenats went to live at Links Road – all a tad confusing but that's life ☺.

At the age of five, Graham followed his sister Winifred to Braintcroft Junior School in Warren Road, Neasden. He was always a gauche, solitary child who had an uncomfortable relationship with his father, but he seemed fond of his stepmother and sister and the family budgerigar 'Lemon'. His family had no serious concern until bottles of chemicals, even Molly's nail varnish, began to vanish – he was now aged nine.

When studying serial killers, one rarely gets to understand where, in their narrative, their psychopathy starts to manifest, however, with Young we are lucky. He passed the 11-plus exam and his father rewarded him with a chemistry set and a place at John Kelly Secondary School in Willesden. He acted well as The Ugly Sister in a pantomime, but being a brooding lad, he was increasingly bored by any subject outside his own obsession. He told other boys that his dad was strict, mean with money and made him sit out the pub while his stepmother played the accordion inside.

Aged 11, Young was regularly borrowing library books on poison and medicine. His stepmother once found a bottle of acid hidden in his school jacket and Graham also enjoyed sniffing ether. When questioned, he told her that he'd stolen it from a chemist's dustbin.

While it is perfectly normal for young children to idolise certain individuals, famous sportsmen, celebrities or even older friends and family members, but he chose some rather unlikely figures as his boyhood role models. He voraciously read books about murderers such as Dr. Crippen and he would pore over a book in the *Sixty Famous Trials* series, which told the story of William Palmer, the Victorian doctor who poisoned his wife and several others with antimony.

Graham then started to read books on Adolf Hitler and the Nazi movement and liked to wear the Nazi swastika on his jacket to school which disturbed the teachers. By the age of twelve he would tell anyone who would listen about his admiration for Adolf Hitler and how the Nazi leader was a much-maligned figure. Soon after that, he began boasting about his interest in the occult and claimed to be part of a local coven run by a man he had met in the local library.

'None of us took this obsession too seriously,' his sister Winifred was to write in her book, *Obsessive Poisoner* (1973). 'We just thought he was plain daft.' Yet, circa this time he started spending his pocket money on poisons, telling a somewhat lax local chemist, Geoffrey Reis, that he was 17 years old – the minimum age back then. In April 1961, he brought 25 grains of antimony, enough to kill several people. 'I was convinced by his knowledge that he was older than he appeared,' Reis, said limply later on.

Young later moved to another chemist for his supplies of lethal substances, signing the poisons register 'M.E. Evans' and began carrying a bottle of antimony with him to school. 'It gave him a sense of security,' one classmate, Clive Creager, recalled. 'He was dangerous. He was evil and I was afraid of him.'

Young's lust for secret power led him to read about black magic and experimented with gunpowder extracted from fireworks. One day, his stepmother found in his jacket a wax model bristling with pins, a symbol of malicious will... Both family and classmates recall his sinister drawings. 'I would be hanging from gallows over a vat of acid,' Creager said. 'Graham would be holding a flame to the rope. He liked drawing people on gallows with syringes marked 'poison' sticking into them. By 1961, Young had become an expert on poisons, their effects, and symptoms. He kept poison bottles at school and books on crime and poison at home which he read and re-read vividly. 'Graham was totally obsessed,' Creager said. 'He had no normal school life, no interest in anything else.'

During the summer of 1961, a strange virus started spreading through the young's home. Since that February, Molly had suffered vomiting, diarrhoea and excruciating stomach pain which were initially dismissed as bilious attacks. Before long Mr. Young Sr, then aged 44, was also suffering with similar stomach cramp, debilitating him for days at a time. Then sister Winifred, now aged 22, was violently ill that summer. Shortly afterwards, Graham was violently sick at home. It also seemed that the mystery bug had spread beyond their household because a couple of Graham's school pals had also been off school ill a couple of times with similar symptoms, then, in November 1961, the plot thickened.

Winifred was served a cup of tea by her brother one morning but found its taste so sour after one mouthful she threw it away. An hour later on the train to work she began to hallucinate and had to be helped out of the station and taken to a hospital where doctors came to the conclusion, she had somehow been infected with the rare poison Belladonna. She told her father Fred who developed a theory; his son had been crazy about chemistry for some years and had even been banned from using chemicals in the house after an experiment set fire to furniture in his room. 'Could the inadvertently contaminated the family food?' he asked himself. He confronted his son. Graham blamed Winifred, claiming she'd been using the family's teacups to mix her shampoo. Unconvinced, Fred searched his son's room but found nothing incriminating, nevertheless, he warned his son to be more careful in the future and 'stop messing around with those bloody chemicals'.

The family had now been concerned about Graham for some while. He was just different, utterly unlike any other boys his age. Since the age of 9 and 10 when he started stealing his stepmother's perfume and nail varnish remover to analyse the contents and sniff the vapours he had been obsessed with chemistry and poisons. If a member of the family took a headache tablet or some cough medicine, he would take immense pleasure in telling the exact scientific names for all the ingredients, and seemed especially keen to tell them, in detail, what agonies would befall them if they took a very large dose. Still a boy has to have a hobby so when he'd scraped through his 11-plus exam, which in those days determined if a kid went on to a grammar school for the more academically minded children, or a secondary modern for those with a more practical bent, his father bought him that chemistry set as a reward. However, Fred was not to know that by this stage of his son's self-education it was the equivalent of giving a cordon bleu chef, a few pots and a beginner's cookbook. With the help of library books, Graham had already gained the knowledge of a chemistry post-graduate, yet his do-it-yourself chemistry experiments were a touch more extreme than you might expect even from the most inquisitive schoolboy. He'd graduated from nail varnish remover to inhaling from a bottle of ether to get high. He carried a bottle of acid around with him which burned a hole in his school blazer. On other occasions he would extract gunpowder from fireworks to make small bombs. He blew up his neighbour's wall and hut but managed to escape blame for the incident. Although Fred and never been particularly close to his son, even he couldn't entertain the idea that his own flesh and blood could be deliberately poisoning the family. If he had only known how his wife's symptoms would worse a few months later, he might have had second thoughts.

Several of Graham's schoolfriends thought him as creepy; that he would try to get them to sniff ether vapours and join him in occult ceremonies, on one occasion sacrificing a neighbourhood cat. In fact, around that time several local cats went missing, suggesting that this was by no means a unique incident.

Although Winifred Young writes in her book *Obsessive Poisoner* that Graham grew to enjoy a close and affectionate relationship with his stepmother, Molly, the boy himself often told classmates how much he hated her. He would show them a small, plasticine voodoo doll full of pins which he carried around saying that it represented Molly. Later, he told psychiatrists how he dreamed how happy his life might have been if only his real mother had lived. Yet, part of this resentment might simply have been the fact that Molly was a strict parent to Graham; she had confiscated a dead mouse he had poisoned, and he drew a picture of a tombstone on which he wrote the words, 'In hateful Memory of Molly Young. RIP'. He then deliberately left it out where she would see it.

Yet Molly young was not the first subject of his life-dangering experiments with poison. His interest in toxicology had helped him befriend a fellow chemistry student, a boy called Christopher Williams, who was also a neighbour of the young family. The pair would often eat their packed lunches together at school and sometimes swap sandwiches. Before long, Williams started to suffer regular bouts of sickness, headaches, and painful cramps. Mrs. Williams didn't know what to think, perhaps it was case of childish play acting. Doctors could only suggest that his symptoms were consistent with severe migraines. The possibility that one of Christopher's schoolfriends was trying to poison him was so far-fetched it had not crossed their minds. Both lads were 13 years old and far too young to buy poisons, however, what they didn't account for was the exceptional cunning of Christopher's new friend Graham who had already purchased from two separate local chemists enough antimony, arsenic, digitalis and Thallium to kill 300 people. Still, he was quite restrained in the doses he gave to Christopher Williams, and they even seemed to have a motive in some cases. For instance, on one occasion Christopher told Graham that he was taking a girl who they both liked out on a date to a TV recording that Friday evening. Conveniently for young, Williams was violently ill that day, so Graham went in his place. Still, even though the pair once had a playground fight with young vowing 'I will kill you for this,' Williams never suspected that his friend's obsession with poisons had anything to do with his recurring illness – besides Graham did a good impression of concern but secretly watched his friend's extreme discomfort with great satisfaction, expressing his sympathies while pondering on the next step Christopher's illness would take. With friends like, who needs enemies?

Here we find a teenage sadist in Graham Young…it was all very well to make his school pals sick, but he needed to watch them closely to try and understand how their symptoms developed, and he couldn't do this in their own homes. Thus, his observations would be made in his own house.

Molly's illness got progressively worse during the early months of 1962. She lost weight, suffered excruciating backache and her hair began to fall out. She also appeared to age noticeably. Winifred later wrote: 'It looked as if she was wasting away in front of our eyes.' When Molly Young woke up on Easter Sunday 1962, however, her symptoms seemed different. Her neck felt stiff, and she had pins and needles in her hands and feet. Nevertheless, she went out shopping, but returned before lunchtime, with Fred out at the local pub When he came home to find his son staring out of the kitchen window watching awestruck as his stepmother writhed in agony in the back garden. She dies in hospital later that day.

Molly Young was cremated at Graham's suggestion after the pathologist concluded that death was due to the prolapse of a bone at the top of her spinal column. This is a known symptom of long-term antimony poisoning yet no connection was made. The most popular conclusion amongst the family was that the injury was connected to a bus crash she was involved in the previous year when she received a blow to the head. It turned out that problem with the spinal column was probably not the cause of death. It is said that Graham had changed his choice of poison after a year of her being regularly dosed Molly had developed a tolerance to antimony and on the evening on the day before she died, he spiked her meal with 20 grains of the colourless, odourless, tasteless heavy metal substance, Thallium. In fact, he rather overdid it, that was enough to kill five or six people.

Even after Molly's death, the family's illness appeared to be spreading. Graham's Uncle John (elsewhere he is called 'Frank') vomited copiously after the funeral – it must have been something he ate, such as the pre-spiked mustard pickle provided for the sandwiches which only Uncle John ate.

By this time, Young's second experimental murder was well underway, and this time the victim was his own flesh and blood. Fred young had suffered the same symptoms as Molly throughout her illness, however after her death Fred's symptoms intensified to the point that he became convinced that he was about to die. When he was admitted to the hospital Graham visited him and enthusiastically discussed his condition with the doctors who couldn't work out if was arsenic or antimony poisoning. The latter was eventually diagnosed, and doctors estimated that one more dose could have killed him. Fred Young later reflected that his bouts of sickness always seemed to happen on a Monday the day after Graham would accompany him to the local pub on Sundays. While that thought only struck him after his son's arrest, during his time in hospital Fred told his daughter not to bring Graham to see him anymore. But still, Fred could bring himself to believe that his 14-year-old son was trying to torture and kill his own family and some friends, was out of the question let alone voice in public, so it fell to a more less emotionally detached figure to try figure things out and rise the alarm.

Graham's school chemistry teacher Jeffrey Hughes had become alarmed about the extreme experiments Young insisted on performing, so one night after school he searched the boy's desk. After finding bottles of poisons, drawings of dying men and essays about famous poisoners, Hughes contacted the police. To try and ascertain his mental state, Graham was sent to what he thought was a career interview, but in reality, the interviewer, a police psychiatrist, appealed to his vanity and persuaded him to talk at length about his expertise with poisons. After the 'careers officer' reported his horrified findings, police officers stepped in and Graham denied everything even when a vial of antimony that he carried around with him and which he referred to as 'my little friend', fell from his shirt pocket. Eventually though, he broke down and confessed all; finally leading police to his several caches of poison stashed in a hedge at home and in the same hut across the road which he'd once blown a hole in with his gunpowder experiments. 'It grew on me like a drug habit', he said of his murderous hobby, 'except it is not me who is taking the drugs.'

Despite the fact that there was insufficient evidence to try the 14-year-old Young for the murder of his stepmother, he was convicted of poisoning his father, his sister and Chris Williams, and found that the was a lack of moral sense being part of his personality. These days we might be tempted to label these traits as 'psychopathic'. He was sent to Broadmoor maximum security hospital with an order that he was not to be released without the permission of the Home Secretary for 15 years.

While on remand awaiting trial, Young was already telling psychiatrists, 'I miss my antimony. I miss the power it gives me. Where's the will though, there's a way.'

Inside Broadmoor, Graham Young was given a small room to himself in the reception block of the gaunt Victorian building, whose redbrick walls sealed off its 750 inmates from the villages of Berkshire.

The window in his room was barred and the bed was screwed to the floor which was bare except for a rug. The 14-year-old was awoken each morning at 7 a.m. and the lights in the block were switched off at 8 p.m. In the intervening hours, he and other inmate/patients made rugs and were allowed to read and play games such as snooker and billiards. Young was one of the three youngest males sent to Broadmoor that century, indeed he was the youngest since 1885. His notoriety had spread throughout the place, and his family felt it was important not to abandon him.

Fred Young tried gamely to conceal his revulsion and anger but, after a few visits, the pair would sit in brood silence, so Fred decided to never again return. His son had not only poisoned Molly, but left Fred Young with a painful liver complaint.

Winifred and Aunt Winnie, however, made regular visits. So did John Walker, the uncle who had become ill at the reception after Molly's funeral. Young constantly asked John to bring him matches. His uncle obliged, until he learnt that they contained phosphorus which can create poisonous effects.

On 6 August 1962, one month after Young arrived at Broadmoor, an inmate called John Berridge suffered convulsions and died with a few hours. This was the same John Berridge that Graham had complained about in letters to Winifred expressing irritation at his loud snoring in the communal dorms.

A post-mortem examination traced the cause to cyanide poisoning. An inquiry found that there was nothing containing this lethal substance inside Broadmoor but that laurel bushes from which it can be extracted, grew alongside the building. Several patients came forward falsely claiming to have murdered Berridge, the authorities, however, were aware that mentally disturbed people often admit to crimes of which they are innocent, investigated each confession closely and were unconvinced that any was true.

But many inmates and some of the nursing staff were privately convinced by one of the confessions. It was made by Graham Young, who spoke in reverent scientific tones of the method of extracting cyanide from laurel leaves – Prunus laurocerasus 'Cherry laurel'.

Exact details of how Young was medically treated still remain confidential. But it is known that, like so many new inmates, he suffered severe depressions and rages during the first year and was given sedatives, sometimes forcibly. These made him put on wight and lose colour and often left him sometimes too dazed to speak clearly. Indeed, early on, his father signed a form allowing the authorities to give his son electroconvulsive therapy, but there is no sign that it was administered. Graham is believed to have disliked group therapy, preferring more personal contact with the psychiatrists. Many of the nurses, though sceptical that Young was becoming 'cured', felt tender pity for him – a youth separated so early from his family.

Young's room at Broadmoor was soon covered with pictures of Nazi war leaders. According to *Murder Casebook* Vol: 59, he grew a clipped

Hitler-style moustache and spent long periods reciting his hearo's war speeches. On the tins provided for tea and sugar, he drew skulls and crossbones and wrote the names of poisons on the labels.

Broadmoor's library was freely available to Young. He selected medical books, from which he broadened his knowledge of poisons and general medicine. He also read William Shirer's *The Rise and Fall of the Third Reich*, one of the standard works of Nazism, as well as Dennis Wheatley's chilling novels about the occult and Bram Stoker's *Dracula*.

Occasionally, Young would amble down to the sports field but never played and used the handicraft centre mainly to make swastikas. He wore on a chain around his neck, sometimes kissing it like a crucifix purely to upset people – enter the shrinks.

The superintendent of Broadmoor, Dr. Patrick McGrath, and a senior resident psychiatrist, Dr. Edgar Udwin, jointly handled young's treatment. The South African-born Dr. Udwin, who ran his own clinic for mentally handicapped children, worked hard to help Young believe that his life was not written off and that he might even go on to study at university. Knowing what we know now and what police and the hospital staff knew back then, one wonders if Dr. Unwin was living on the same planet as us sane human beings. Nonetheless, the nursing staff were torn between its suspicion of Young and a wish to avoid making him an outcast among outcasts – something he was happily doing anyway. And, yes, here is more good news: he was given a job in the kitchen – ye, the KITCHEN for fuckkk's sake…the understatement that this was a 'risk', but a 'gesture of trust' they felt Young needed. And no prizes for getting what happened next. Shortly afterwards, the nurse's coffee was served looking unusually dark. It was found to contain Harpic toilet bleach.

No one was harmed, but the nurses learned to joke with troublesome inmates: 'Unless you behave, I'll let Graham make your coffee.'

'He lived very much in a fantasy world at first…all he could talk about were his poisons.'

Late in 1965, after only three years in Broadmoor, Young applied for release. His father begged the authorities never to set him free ever again, but young's case was weak anyway, and was rejected. Soon after, a two packets of tea sugar soap used to wash down walls before painting, went missing and ended up in the communal tea urn. Potentially 97 people could have had their stomach's burned out and might well have died. Young was sent to the maximum-security block, known there as 'The Cooler'.

Finally defeated, Young came to realise that he had to cooperate if he was ever to be released. Dr. Udwin noticed gradual changes in Young after his release from the cooler and for the next three years, Young showed signs of becoming steadier, more responsive to others, with Dr. Udwin not even realising that this young psychopath was playing the long game.

Young talked less and less to Doc Udwin about poisons, although the psychiatrist was aware that the youth continued to admire the Nazi policy of exterminating Jews. It is not known if Young realised that Dr. Udwin was himself a Jew, and the years passed slowly. Young, weathered jibs from other inmates that he was the doctors' 'blue-eyed boy' and even before his release was considered, he applied for work in the police forensic laboratories, and for a place on the Pharmaceutical Society training scheme - the actions of someone who lives in a world where lead balls bounce, pink elephants fly and fairies reign supreme. With both applications thrown into the waste bin, Young now wrote to the National Front and 'Column 88' a fascist moment and was accepted as a member. He was entitled to his views, however right-wing, and in June 1970, Dr. Udwin reported to the Home Office that Young had undergone - profound changes', and that his obsession with poison and violence had passed.

Criminals who have been committed to mental hospitals often face longer periods of confinement than criminals receiving prison terms. There is no automatic system of parole. In order to be released, restricted patients have to be authorised by the Home Secretary or by a Mental Health Review Tribunal. The Home Secretary will take advice from the Regional Medical Officer as well as a special committee consisting of a lawyer, a psychiatrist, and a social worker. If the Home Secretary fails to recommend release, the person can apply directly to the Mental Health Review Tribunal and may keep doing this every 12 month if his application is refused or till the cows come home. If the Tribunal authorises a discharge, it will take one or two forms – either absolute or conditional. In the latter case, a patient generally remains subject to recall to the hospital for the rest of his or her life.

Young, nearing his 23rd birthday, was delighted and, on 16 June, he wrote to tell Winifred, now married and living in Hemel Hempstead, that 'the estimable Edgar' hoped to discharge him later that year, add 'your friendly Frankenstein is soon to be released.'

None of the family knew a release was being considered but they understood that the Home Office could overrule the original sentence on psychiatrists' recommendation. Fred Young, now living in Sheerness, Kent, was dismayed but Winifred and her husband Dennis Shannon, were assured by Dr. Udwin that her brother was cured, thus on 21 November, Young began a week's stay with them. It passed well, and in a quiet moment, he expressed remorse for what he had done. He returned at Christmas, bringing presents and a card stating that their dog had received psychoanalysis and was well again. It was signed 'Sigmund Freud'. And then he started ranting on about 'The Final Solution' suggesting that this might solve the problems of 'The Troubles' in Northern Ireland which were going on.

Early in 1971, Home Secretary Reginald Maudling authorised the Home Office to release Young, proving he accepted conditions about treatment and a fixed address. On 4 February, Young walked free, only a few weeks after telling a nurse, 'When I get out, I'm going to kill one person for every year I've spent in this place.' Apparently, this very revealing comment never reached the ears of the authorities despite being taken down on file at the time.

One of the first things Graham Young did upon his release was to make a sentimental journey to visit the two chemists where he had previously obtained his poisons and proudly announced his name there to see if his notoriety had stood the test of time. He. Even returned to his former family home in Neasden introducing himself to neighbours he had known as a teenager. He even visited his old schoolmaster; tellingly he seemed most keen to remind them of his notorious past crimes than to boast about his rehabilitation.

Within a week of his release, Young attended a Government Training Centre in Slough to begin training as a storekeeper and moved into a hostel nearby. Soon after his arrival, though, a fellow hostel 'friend' Trevor Sparkes,

34, complained of severe abdominal pains and a loss of control of his legs, but the doctor could find nothing wrong. 'This might help,' Young said, offering keen footballer Sparkes a glass of wine that evening. Sparkes drank it and immediately suffered vomiting, facial swelling, diarrhoea, strange scrotal pains, and near-convulsions which recurred throughout April, saying that he suffered 'diabolical pains years afterward', and he never played soccer again.

Around the same time, another man claimed to have had a drink in 'The Eagle' pub on Slough's High Street with an intense young man obsessed with poisons, later committed suicide. It was never proven that in any way Young was the cause of this man's agonies and subsequent passing.

Earlier that month, Fred Young received an official visitor from Broadmoor, who explained that his son's release was under consideration. Given that Young had already been released and had had a frosty meeting with his father, Fred was outraged at the bureaucratic incompetence at Broadmoor and stupidity of his misinformed visitor.

In mid-April, Young saw an advertisement for a storekeeper at a firm in Bovingdon, Hertfordshire, a village four miles from his sister's home. John Hadland Ltd, specialised in high-speed photographic and optical equipment. 'I previously studied chemistry, organic and inorganic pharmacology and toxicology...' Young wrote in his application letter. When Young arrived for his interview on 23 April, the managing director, Godfrey Foster, had received the Slough Centre's glowing report on the young man, who was eager to talk about science. Foster, however, was more curious about the obvious gaps in young's history. Young, lied, explaining that he had suffered a nervous breakdown after his mother had died in an accident, but was now fully recovered. Foster, still unsure, said he would be in touch when he had made a decision. He then wrote to Slough asking for a personal reference from young's psychiatrist.

On 26 April, the Centre forwarded Dr. Udwin's report. It was written on Broadmoor or Home Office stationery but did not conceal the seriousness of Young's disturbance. 'This man has suffered a deep-going personality disorder which necessitated his hospitalisation throughout the whole of his adolescence,' Dr. Udwin's letter began. 'He has, however, made an extremely full recovery and is now entirely fit for discharge, his sole disability now being the need to catch up with his lost time.' No mention of his erstwhile predilections for poisons, which might have been relevant considering highly toxic chemicals were used on the company's premises, but to have done so would have ruined Young's prospect of a worthwhile job.

Foster duly accepted the report in all good faith and offered £24 a week to Young who wrote the following flowery letter to his new employer:

'I am pleased to accept your offer, and the conditions attached, thereto, and shall, therefore, report on Monday, May 10th, at 8.30 a.m.

'May I take this opportunity to express my gratitude to you for offering me this position, notwithstanding my previous infirmity as communicated to you by the Placing Officer. I shall endeavour to justify your faith in me by performing my duties in an efficient and competent manner.'

Until Monday next week, I am,

Yours Faithfully,

GRAHAM YOUNG.'

At 8.30 a.m. on Monday 10 May, Young turned up for his first day at John Hadland Ltd.'s Newhouse Laboratories dressed smartly in suit and tie. Fortunately, Young did not have to avail himself of the toxic substances kept on site; he had already been to London armed with the fake ID, 'M.E. Evans' that he'd used as a teenager and bought a new batch of antimony potassium tartrate, the full name he insisted on calling it, from John Bell and Croydon, and in his most scholarly form and showed the senior dispenser, Albert Kearne, some notepaper headed 'Bedford College – part of London University. He then called upon Freeman Grieve in St. Albans to get hold of Thallium. (Both chemists were later fined for failing to comply with the existing laws governing the sale of poisons.)

The first workmate Young made friends with was 44-year-old Ron Hewitt who was due to leave the firm but would stay on a for a few weeks to show him the ropes so he could take over his job.

Hadland' staff welcomed Young. Some quickly felt protective towards the rather solitary, absent-minded young man. The 59-year-old storeroom manager, Bob Egle, tried to take Young under his wing, as did 60-year-old Fred Biggs, who was head of the Work in Progress Unit.

Bob Egle was a benign, tolerant man. He had been married to his wife Dorothy for 38 years and the couple lived in Chesham, Hertfordshire, but planned to retire to Norfolk to be near their daughter. During Egle's army days, he had been in action in the Dunkirk evacuation of 1940. Young loved to ply him with questions about his war experiences.

Fred Biggs was a parttime employee at Hadland's, in charge of stocks and distribution. He and his wife Annie lived in the nearby village of Chipperfield, where he had formerly run the village store. Annie and Fred had won many ballroom dancing titles, and Fred represented his village on a rural council. Like Egle, Biggs often lent Young cigarettes or money for his bus fare.

Another storeroom worker, Jethro Batt, drove Young back to his digs every night, but others among the 75 employees found their new colleague a bit obsessive. He seemed at peace only when discussing his beloved Adolf Hitler. Nevertheless, Young seemed keen to reciprocate the goodwill. He handed around his rolled-up cigarettes and offered to fetch tea for his fellow workers from Mrs Bartlett's trolley. This was left each morning outside the storeroom where he worked.

Initially, Young stayed with Winifred and Dennis in Hemel Hempstead but soon moved to a bedsitting room at 29 Maynard Road in the town for £4 a week. The owners, Mr Saddiq and his family had house rules, one of which tenants were not allowed to use the kitchen – a very lucky restriction as it turned out for them, indeed, no cooking was allowed and he ate most of his evening meals at a nearby Wimpy place, but twice a week he visited Winifred for a decent bite to eat.

After a time, Egle started to take off time because he was all and spend a few days in bed with a stomach upset. On 8 March, soon after drinking his tea from the trolley, Ron Hewitt, who discussed science with young suffered sharp stomach pains, diarrhoea, and burning sensation in in his throat after drinking a cup of tea brought to him by Young. The symptoms lasted a few days, but the doctors could only suggest food poisoning or gastric flu. Hewitt was back at work by 15 June, still shaken and weak, and the attacks continued for the next three weeks, invariably after drinking tea and over the following three weeks he suffered no fewer than 12 bouts of this mysterious illness – always immediately after drinking tea yet he never suspected a thing – yet after leaving the company the symptoms completely disappeared.

Bob Egle also fell ill; feeling fragile he took a week's holiday in Great Yarmouth with his wife Dorothy from 18 June. Since Fred Biggs was on his scheduled summer holiday, the storeroom was short-staffed and Young became a little bit bossy. However, the day after Egle returned to work feeling much better and saying: Nothing like a bit of sea air', his fingers became numb and he couldn't move with agonising pain, at night he lay awake moaning. In the morning, Egle's doctor had him taken to West Herts Hospital, which soon transferred him to the intensive care unit at St. Albans City Hospital. The numbness spread throughout his body until, in agony he was almost paralysed yet still able to hear but not speak. The specialists revived him twice when his heart stopped but finally there was nothing more they could do. To the horror his workmates, on Wednesday, 7 July 1971, with his wife at his bedside, Bob Egle died. Cause of death was officially 'Bronchial Pneumonia' and polyneuritis arising Guillain- Barré syndrome, a very rare and serious condition that affects the feet, hands, and limbs. Throughout Egle's final weeks, Young had constantly asked Godfrey Foster's secretary about his condition and had once shown her a medical article about polyneuritis, and saying the symptoms were similar to those Egle was suffering and still no one suspected anything! 'It's terribly said,' said Young, 'that Bob went through the terrors of Dunkirk only to fall victim to such a strange virus.

Such was Young's concern over Bob's death, Foster chose him to represent the storeroom staff at Egle's cremation at Amersham on 12 July. He spent the entire journey in Foster's car talking about polyneuritis, specifically the Guillain- Barré syndrome which Egle was determined at post mortem to have suffered – yet Foster never suspected a thing, but did he?

During the weeks following Egle's death, staff at Hadland tried to put the tragic incident behind them yet the rather workshy young storeman insisted on musing about the possible cause of Bob Egle's bizarre symptoms.

In the autumn, Young was promoted to be put in charge of the storeroom for a trial period. He had become a more outgoing person but irritated some staff by talking constantly about the much-mourned Bob Egle. He managed his new responsibility badly, and his obsession with the Nazis was another source of his growing unpopularity. He kept in contact with his family; besides the visits to Winifred and Winnie, he visited his cousin in St. Albans and quite often went to Sheerness where Fred and Aunt Winnie were cheered by his relative success at work. The family had heard about Bob Egle but realised that men approaching 60 were susceptible to pneumonia.

Early in September 1971, Fred Biggs also began to suffer violent stomach cramps, vomiting and other symptoms, and he wasn't the only one. Hadland's import-export manager, Peter Buck, had a cup of tea with Young and a clerk named David Tilson. 15-minutes later, Tilson felt ill after a tea-break and two days later felt his legs going numb. The following Friday, 15 October, Young and 39-year-old fellow storeman, Jethro Batt, were working late together. 'Do you know, Jeth, it is quite easy to poison someone and make it look like natural causes?' Young asked, prattling on about something he called a 'recipe for death'. While Batt was out of the room, Young made some coffee. Batt found the first mouthful bitter and threw the rest away. 'What's the matter?' Young asked. 'Do you think I'm trying to poison you?' They both laughed. Twenty-minutes later, Batt was sick. Over the weekend, his legs throbbed with pain, yet he did not suspect a thing!

On Monday, 18 October, Tilson was admitted to St. Albans City Hospital suffering pains throughout his body. Within a few hours his hair began to fall out. Batt, still in bed at home, felt the pain up to his chest.

During the week at Hadland, Young handed a mug to a woman colleague, 39-year-old Diane Smart. 'This is your coffee, Di. Drink it up.' Minutes later, she vomited, and cramp spread through her hands, legs and stomach.

Jethro Batt, meanwhile, was so tormented by pain at home that he told his wife he wanted to die. He suffered hallucinations and his hair, like Tilson's, began to fall out. Painkillers brought no relief. By Thursday, 21 October, Batt could scarcely move. A week later, Tilson left hospital but returned in distress on 1 November. The doctors had last seen him with long hair. Now he was almost bald. On 5 November, Batt also entered hospital almost without a hair on his head, and still no one suspected a thing!

'I am most annoyed. He is surviving far too long for my peace of mind.'
Graham Young, diary entry 1971, on Fred Biggs.

Young went in to work on Saturday, 6 November, to catch up on work and was joined by Fred Biggs, whose latest attack had only just passed. Young made tea for Biggs, but Godfrey Foster cancelled his own request for tea when told the work was done. The next day, Biggs had a relapse.

Bless him, Foster suspected that a well-known recurring virus, known as the 'Bovingdon Bug' was causing the outbreak. Some employees wondered about the radioactive experiments on a nearby disused airstrip. Others feared the water was somehow contaminated

The doctors treating Hadland's. staff were perplexed. Biggs was examined by no less than seven doctors after entering West Herts Hospital on 4 November, but they were unable to pinpoint the cause of his suffering. On 11 November, he was moved to the Whittington Hospital, which specialises in viral complaints, but rather than getting better, his skin began to peel off.

On the same day, at Foster's request, the factory was examined by Dr. Robert Hynd, the Medical Officer of Health for Hemel Hempstead, and a team of factory inspectors. They found nothing amiss. Hynd returned the next day to question the anxious staff separately about any illness in their families.

Fred Biggs was then transferred to the National Hospital for Nervous Diseases in London, again to no avail. On Friday, 19 November, he died. 'I wonder what went wrong,' Young told Diane Smart. 'He shouldn't have died. I was very fond of Fred.'

With his workforce close to panic, the proprietor, John Hadland' summoned the firm's GP, Dr Iain Anderson, to address everyone in the canteen. Dr. Anderson explained that there was no radioactive contamination from the airstrip and there was no heavy metal poisoning. Thallium, a heavy metal chemical, was sometimes used in making high refractive lenses, but by Hadland's. he said, reassuringly, that there must have been an unusually virulent outbreak of the Bovingdon Bug and that intensive efforts were being made to trace its origin. While Young sniggered quietly, the doctor pleaded for calm. Then John Hadland invited questions. 'Why had heavy metal been ruled out?' someone asked from the back. It was Graham Young.

Dr. Anderson repeated what the factory inspectors had decided. He privately suspected that some heavy metal might still be found to be the cause…the net was slowly starting to encircle Graham Young, who, with his oversized ego, continued to press more probing questions. 'So are you an expert on toxicology, doctor? I think not but I *AM*,' he snapped. Eventually, Hadland declared the meeting closed. Dr. Anderson casually went to see Young in the storeroom and flattered him on his knowledge. As always, Young warmed to appreciation and took the opportunity to parade his knowledge of poisons. 'Goodness, me,' Dr. Anderson exclaimed. 'You are, I think, in the wrong job, a highly-intelligent young man like you. Have you considered a career in medicine? I would certainly help you get your foot in the door.' Young beamed.

After this informal chat, the doctor reported back to John Hadland with his suspicions. Both were reluctant to take action without proof. But when left alone, Hadland thought matters over. He telephoned the police.

'I had ceased to see them as people or, more correctly, a part of me had.
They became guinea pigs.'
Graham Young on his victims to DCS Ronald Harvey, Head of Hertfordshire
CID.

Sadly, as much as I ache for it, there is no word count room in this chapter or book to document the subsequent police investigation; Young's arrest at his father's home on 21 November 1971, the exhumation of Fred Biggs for toxicology tests, and his trial after which he was sentenced to serve life in prison, for all of these issues can be found elsewhere. It is the matter of his release from Broadmoor that should concern us all, even retrospectively.

'Of all murderers, the poisoner is the foulest,' wrote Fryniwyd Tennyson Jesse Hardwood (1888-1958) in *Murder and its Motives* (1924). An English criminologist, journalist, and author, she was the second of three daughters of the Reverend Eustace Tennyson D'Eyncourt Jesse and Edith

James, and a great-niece of the poet Alfred, Lord Tennyson, and she certainly knew her stuff with penmanship in her blood. She added: 'He [the poisoner] must have the confidence of the person he/she is killing; must be appear amiable, pleasant,' and way back when she wrote those words she might as well have been writing about Graham Young, in an 'if the cap fits, wear it' sort of way.

With that in mind, family and colleagues recoiled from the obvious fact that Young was intentionally poisoning them. He knew how to exploit the doubt and decency of people who chose not to accuse without proof. He made them feel guilty simply for suspecting he was a criminal because, as Tennyson Jesse wrote: 'The poisoner undermines the whole fabric of trust on which society rests.' Even John Hadland rang his solicitor before telephoning the police. Young played along with other peoples' image of himself: his family saw a gauche boy who had never known his birth mother; chemists saw a scholar; the Broadmoor psychiatrists saw a maturing personality and potential 'success story', and oh, boy, did the shrinks get it all BIG TIME wrong. Young was a homicidal psychopath, he knew their weaknesses, yet still the psychiatrists, the entire British criminal justice system, and just about every medical evaluation board, didn't get it either, for he, like all other homicidal psychopathic individuals, are the consummate control freaks and they CANNOT be cured, and the *Sunday Times* bestselling book *Talking with Psychopaths: A Journey into the Evil Mind*, documents case after case where those in whom we place our complete trust to evaluate a criminal's state of mind, and to protect you, me, our children, and our loved ones from their predations, have got it big time wrong too.

So, I ask where is the accountability here? Yes, the two chemists who supplied Young with toxic substances were fined. But, what about the total incompetence of Dr. Udwin and Dr. McGrath, when they and many of the hospital's staff knew, 100 percent, that they had a Nazi-loving poisoner in their facility but allowed him to work in the kitchen? He was filling the communal tea urn with Harpic for God's sake, and they still didn't cotton on. Did Young tell staff that he intended to kill a person for every year that he'd been in Broadmoor? Yes, he did, but still he was rubber-stamped by Dr. Udwin as having '…made an extremely full recovery and is now entirely fit for discharge, his sole disability now being the need to catch up with lost time.'

Without seeming to be obtuse, ummm, and why not, yes Dr. Udwin, whom Young called 'My Edgar, certainly caught up on his lost time only weeks after you allowed recommended his release, despite the fact that he was reading, aged 12 and 13, amongst other books, John Rowland's *Poisoner in the Dock*, which admirably handled the infamous William Palmer, of Rugeley, Staffordshire.

Later, Professor Hugh Molesworth-Johnson actually consulted the Agatha Christie book – *The Pale Horse*, which Young had read time and again in Broadmoor. It was Prof. Hugh who performed the post-mortem examination on one of Young's victims in 1972, the book being mentioned at trial. Agatha Christie's husband, Max Mallowan, was later to say that his wife would have been 'deeply distressed' if any criminal had benefited from the material in her books.

After his trial, Young was taken to HMP Wormwood Scrubs in London, later to be transferred to HMP Parkhurst, a maximum-security facility on the Isle of Wight. In January 1973, the inquiry into the Young case, headed by the Recorder of London, Sir. Cecil Carl Aavold, published its finding that Young had been 'released in accordance with the procedures accepted at that time.' NOTE: Still no accountability levelled against those who allowed this compulsive poisoner to kill again and again.

On 1 October 1975, a second inquiry, led by Lord Butler, published its proposals for sweeping changes to tighten the supervision of all known 'abnormal offenders', both inside and outside prison hospitals. It also called for an independent advisory board (yet *another* pen-pushing quango) to advise the Home Secretary - who are brought into office then kicked out again on an almost yearly basis - on applications for release. The Labour government accepted the proposals and as might be expected, does one sense '*Groundhog Day*' all over again – I do!

With Broadmoor Hospital now deemed so incompetent to handle Graham Young again – which should have been the case from the outset – he was kept in HMP Parkhurst until in early August 1990, when the Home Office announced that he had died after a heart attack at the age of forty-two. He was cremated on the Isle of Wight.

***

Exorcism at Broadmoor.

'Your mother sucks cocks in hell!

The Demon in The Exorcist.

The Exorcist, is the 1973 film directed by William Friedkin starring Linda Blair who played 'Regan', a young girl who was possessed after using a Ouija board. Two priests, one played by William O'Malley attempted to perform an exorcism on her. Harrowing scenes that stick in the mind of many. I am not saying anyone's head in Broadmoor spun round or belched out six meters of sick. Imagine Broadmoor contacting the Vatican to ask if they could perform an exorcism. Former staff have written to me and said '…the worst of the worst and makes others look like saints…'

Michael Taylor, also known as 'The Exorcist Killer ', was placed inside Broadmoor for the murder of his wife in September 1974. A butcher by trade, married to Christine and the father of five children, there was nothing unusual about the 31-year-old, and nothing to suggest that he had problems apart from a back condition. He soon become member of a local fellow Christian group; attending twice a week with his wife and forming a close relationship with a lady called 'Marie'. This did not go unnoticed by the group or Marie's husband who objected to the two sitting together. At the next meeting in July the two men exchanged words, and it became somewhat heated. Taylor apologised and forgiveness was given by him to the group and two days later even Taylor's wife was happy with the outcome. This did not stop Taylor becoming more erratic and unpredictable a few weeks later resulting in the local vicar calling in the big guns to perform what they call a 'deliverance' with a minister to perform a ritual of cleansing. A month had moved on and Taylor seemed to be normal, or as normal as one can be until the night of the 6 October the same year. At approximately 9.45 pm a phone call was taken by West Yorkshire police: '…there is someone running round covered in red paint'. PC Ian Walker was on duty expecting a peaceful night and received the call to attend, the initial response being that this had to be a hoax. Arriving on scene and seeing a male covered in blood from head to foot standing saying nothing, there was Taylor, zombie-like looking with an air of silence not even a whisper from him, PC Walker who only had the customary truncheon unlike today's police officer's, stab vest, taser and a baton, must have felt somewhat out of his depth being alone and faced with a scene from an apocalyptic horror movie. Approaching Taylor who offered no resistance the cop gingerly held out a hand and asked: 'Sir, I must ask you to come with me.' There was no struggle, just a scream from Taylor howling: 'It's the blood of Satan!' PC Walker suspecting something horrendous radioed requested that Taylor's house was visited. The scene upon other officers' arrival was utter carnage and a dog was found hacked to death in the bedroom Taylor's wife was found. A faceless body with a tongue pulled from the throat area along with vast amounts of blood splattered over the walls. When questioned at the police station Taylor could not recall what had happened in the house and he kept on muttering 'It's the blood of Satan'.

What comes to light after all these events was the lead up to the murder. Taylor had begrudgingly joined the church group and had seen Mary allegedly performing an exorcism on a lady called Mavis Taylor believed that this would help him relieve the pain going through his back. This resulted in Taylor becoming besotted with Mary. Taylor was not religious in any way but became close to Mary resulting in them communicating in a secret type of speech and praying together every available time they could. On 1 October Taylor and Mary sat together all-night in the hall praying and making the sign of the cross over each other. Was this the catalyst that forced the church to perform an exorcism on Taylor? From the outset of the exorcism Taylor spat at the two priests involved along with punching and kicking out. The placing of a crucifix and the splashing of Holy water resulted in 30 plus demons being identified as taking over Taylor's body. The result in the morning were the priests warning there was still demons present in Taylor's body.

During the trial Taylor's defence Mr Ognall QC stated. 'Let those who are truly responsible for this killing stand up. We submit that Taylor is a mere, cipher. The real guilt is elsewhere. Religion is the key'.   The Vatican was contacted by Broadmoor to authorise an exorcism of Taylor, so in 1976 the Department of Health must have given the go ahead. Only six people were present this is confirmed by an unnamed warder who was present at the ritual and contacted my website. The Department of Health at the time shockingly using religious beliefs to rid someone of evil? Even today the NHS will not comment or confirm or deny such happenings. Does the NHS consider exorcism a form of treatment? The church do believe exorcism is a form of treatment. What I find astounding is that educated doctors who have studied mental health for years possibly taking to exorcism. But this is not the end of the matter by any means.

Noreen O'Conner.

'I plucked someone's eyeballs out it is not Maria that is dead. It is the evil that was in her eyes.'

Noreen O'Conner upon her arrest.

Somerset the cider drinker's heaven and a county where not much happens that would be considered sinister but think again. In the village of Loxton, Noreen O'Connor, a state registered nurse who took over the job of nursemaid housekeeper for Mrs Emily and Mr Frank Tiarks from a Miss Frederika Alwin Buls, known as Maria, who was German and was interned just as the Second World War broke out. Emily passed away in 1942, but by this time Frank was confined to a wheelchair and housebound due to a hunting accident. O'Connor took to the life in the village like a duck to water, so much so she that helped in the funding and raising of funds for the new school to be based in the local village hall. Attending Sunday Service along with helping the local vicar with fetes and village hall sales, you know the old-fashioned ones where cakes and bakes are available.

Loxton a quaint little village not too far from Weston Super-Mare and Cheddar with a stunning little church called St Andrews. Did you know Loxton takes its name from the Lox Yeo River on which it is situated, and the village gets a mention in the Domesday book as 'Lochestone', neither did I until we started this chapter. For anyone unfamiliar with the Domesday book or the middle English spelling 'Doomsday', the year was 1086 and it was a manuscript record, a bit like today's census and then used to calculate who paid what in land and building tax. Frank was a generous man and a former merchant banker in London; not short of money and from a generous family that can be traced back years in Loxton's history. Frank Tiarks brought an eight-bedroom property called 'Gardeen' in Christon road Loxton and he donated it to O'Conner along with a lump sum of twenty thousand pounds on the death of Frank in 1952 - the equivalent of half a million pounds in today's money. Frank Tiarks often holidayed to South Africa accompanied by O'Conner; she also drove Frank around in a car that was adapted for him. Frank was often seen at the local cricket club watching matches with his help. Noreen O'Connor was a tall lady light coloured shoulder-length hair, smartly dressed and could turn a man's head. Immaculately dressed wearing Dior

Brown Astrakhan coat, and in the same year O'Connor asked Maria who stayed in the UK after the war to move in as this was stipulated by Frank in his will. At 77 years old, frail with a broken leg and having suffered two strokes, Maria needed looking after and soon settled in.

On 1 September 1954, at about 7.20 am O'Conner called the son of her former employer: 'Please come over, something terrible has happened to Marie she's in the power of some evil.' Peter living in Bridport fifty miles away left and set out towards Loxton. Meanwhile the daily help, a Mrs Eva Simmons, had arrived at 8.15 am and had noticed the curtains in Marie's room were closed. O'Conner said to Mrs Simmons 'Something terrible has happened.; Peter arrived on the scene resembling something out of a horror movie: O'Conner stood with Peter over the lifeless body of Maria. O'Connor said to Peter: 'I plucked Marie's eyes out but it's not Marie.' Thereafter, O'Connor was arrested and taken to Weston Super Mare. She was quiet till the evening when police officers noticed she started moving cell furniture then chanting religious sayings. On one occasion she knelt for some time and prayed. A sorry sight and pitiful noise from a broken lady, she had led exemplary life no hint of any trouble or any ill feeling towards anyone. Maureen was taken to Holloway Prison in North London. What turned in a moment in time, what vision or sound did O'Conner see or hear? There were no money motive or any financial worries due to the income from investments and being a director of Callow Rock Lime Company given to her by Frank Tairk, so financial gain was ruled out early on. O'Conner had seen something in Maria's eyes, something so terribly evil and horrific that Noreen O'Conner felt she needed to extinguish.

Mr Justice Byrne was sitting at the Somerset Assize wells on 15 October 1954. During the trial various doctors gave evidence including Dr Thomas

Christie who had observed Noreen in prison. He told the court that in his opinion Miss O' Connor was suffering from acute mania; a condition recognised as a disease of the mind. Another witness Mr Maurice William Bailey a former clerk of the local council along with being a director of Callow Rock Lime Company said he had known O'Connor for a number of years. Bailey also claimed O'Connor was deranged after she had claimed someone had tried to kill her during a road accident some time previously A Dr Desmond Curran a psychiatrist at St George's Hospital, London, and who interviewed O'Connor, agreed with others that it was unlikely that she knew what she was doing. There was no cross-examination of any witness or of Miss O'Connor. The jury took one minute to decide a guilty verdict but insane. The order was given by the judge that O'Connor was to be detained at Broadmoor until her Majesty's pleasure be known.

Mild mannered, polite and a lady who had a moment in time that only she can explain but never did, O'Connor was released to St Andrew's hospital in Northampton a few years later where she died in 1983. During an August day, Chris Berry-Dee and I took a drive to Loxton after contacting Jane Jay who was one of the Warders for St Andrews Church and we found Noreen O'Connor's grave. On the route down in anticipation we were driving through the Mendip Hills with stunning views either side, then a bus, not just a small bus, but a double decker slowed us up. The question was asked by us both; why was a double decker crawling at a snail's pace along a narrow road that even a gnat's arse would have trouble passing? For mile-after-mile, this diesel-belching, lane-hogging public conveyance wound its way uphill, downhill, clogging up the traffic, stopping to let no one get on and no one get off...until … this fuckin' bus stopped once again. For several minutes it stayed put...then...the oldest lady in the whole world was assisted off by the driver. Phew! At last. Thank God. We breathed deep sighs of relief…. but wait for it, wait for it…for the moment the driver moved forward she waved him to stop again…: Jesus Christ…because she had alighted at the wrong stop!

Now I don't know if any of my readers have ever met Chris Berry-Dee; former HM Royal Marines 'Green Beret Commando', allegedly having the patience of 'Saint Patience'; a man of worldly wisdom who does not suffer fools lightly. So, after this 'experience' behind the bus, with the fuel gauge on his V8 Jaguar plummeted south faster than Eddie the Eagle on his ski slope, he looked into my eyes and, and with a hint of pure evil he said in measured tones:

> 'You know what you are Boris. You are a f****g asshole. You *insisted* on being my navigator on this trip, but you forgot your glasses and you can't even read yr phone's SatNav 'an stop turning the fuckin' thing around and upside down. We've gone 40-miles out of our way, and all we have seen so far is the fat ass of a fuckin' BIG bus that has *no right* to be on these lanes in the first place!'

'Oh, well,' I thought secretly to myself, 'If this is what researching true crime is all about, I will bring my glasses along next time', but as a reward I did buy Christopher a pork pie later on…and that turned out to be crap too. Nonetheless, 45-minutes well overdue we met up with church warden Jane and took a short walk along a path that was covered either side by bramble bushes ladened with some sort of fruit, then through a wooden arch and gate. It was stunningly peaceful…so beautiful it took our breath away with the tiny Loxton church just a few yards way. To the left was Noreen's grave, as close to the entrance that you could get and it was an odd feeling and we knew it straightaway: about two meters in length a meter wide and six inches a thick plain slab, just visible are the words 'Noreen O' Connor 1907 to 1983' (the reader can see this on my website www.broadmoorsinister.com, and it had taken me this visit to her grave to establish her precise year of birth. She is buried in the direction given to God-fearing folk and not that of a monster, all proving that she had been dearly loved by everyone who had known her. With that said, our drive back home was interesting as we thought about and discussed the case, and was Frederika Buls possessed? And did Noreen see something from the 'Bottomless Pit' in the eyes of Frederika? Noreen was well thought of and much respected even after the dreadful event in 1954. This quaint village did not turn against her, nor protest at her being buried in the churchyard not far from the house where she had once lived. And I will leave this chapter on a high note. If you are ever passing near Loxton, please go and visit one of the most beautiful little churches in the UK…leave a little something in the collection plate too. Then pay a visit to Noreen's grave to say a private prayer. Christopher, sensing the importance of my visit, had bought some flowers for me to place there. To thank him, I most generously bought him a pork pie from a petrol station! Hey, what more does one expect a Cockney lad to do…eels and chips is stretching things a bit too far don't you think…well I do!

***

Robert Napper.

The research for ANY genre of book, fact or fiction, is great fun as long as one doesn't imagine you are on a guaranteed way to literary riches. It *has* to be a labour of love. As a very strict, no prisoners taken taskmaster, Christopher, has drummed into me, as he has with countless other seriously keen novice writers: you do it because *you want to*…that you are dedicated to putting pen to paper, and let the Devil take the Hindmost. So, it has been a great privilege for me to having been 'tutored' by one of the greatest true crime writers of all time. So here, let's take another example with Robert Napper.

It was a hot sunny day, and on the way back home from filming and this time with me driving, we decided to visit Broadmoor Hospital, and instantly seeing a sign 'No public right of way'. 'Bugger that,' said Christopher', let's wander. It's us common folk who pay for this place to exist,' with him ambling along as the old fellow being a miserable Victor Meldrew that he can be when the mood takes his fancy. So, we made our way downhill passing thirty-foot walls and razor wire. Slowly the view opened up and there it was - Surrey and Hampshire from Berkshire. The gasp from the world's Number One true crime author was a noise to behold and something that will stay with me.

Along the path that split the old hospital gardens to the right was vast lush vegetation with apple trees and pear; an old football pitch that 'Broadmoor United' once played home-and-away games. To the left, unkept and a sorry sight. The trees inside the walled garden were hanging with fruit, apples, and pears along with brambles ladened with berries some ripe. It is hard to imagine who the patients were that have graced these gardens or played on the home pitch. Some whom having committed the worst of the worst crimes while still allowed the peaceful serenity of the gardens. Yes, yes, this is exactly what Christopher has said in his Prologue about 'care' One can still imagine Ronnie Kray standing on the side lines of the football pitch licking his lips at the young ones running around, or Graham Young picking the deadliest plants for his urn of tea.

We often come across heinous crimes and sometimes they have something in common with the way the killer is brought up... childhood abuse; seeing parents fighting or abusing each other can stick in the mind because children's' brains are like sponges they soak in so much and believe sometimes that is the norm to do harm. I am not using this as an excuse to commit crime, murder, rape, nor do I believe on the other hand though it could have an effect, or does it...so 'The Green Chain Rapist' or the 'Plumstead Rapist' is a name that sticks in the mind of many.

Robert Clive Napper could have been arrested in 1989 *if* the police had listened to Napper's mother. Born on the 25 February 1966, in Erith, southeast London, to parents Pauline and Brian Napper along with siblings two brothers and one sister, Napper's father was a driving instructor, his mother a housewife. Beatings by Napper's father upon his mother was constant along with abuse of her. This resulted in divorce in 1974 and the children, all four of them, going to foster parents. Furthermore, it seems Napper was sexual abused by a relative while on a camping trip and this had had a deep impact on his mental state. Napper's mother saw the change in him when he returned to the family home minus the father, and this is one of those long-drawn-out investigations which police could have solved much earlier and prevented. The fact is they just did not listen. Napper admitted to his mother that he had raped a woman on Plumstead common. The police had looked through records and came across no such reported crime by anyone. Coming to light, sometime later a woman was raped in a garden in the close vicinity of Plumstead Common. The woman was a thirty-year-old mother of two children, and she was raped in front of them. Napper's mother soon after disowned her son and refused to have anything to do with him. Napper left her home to live in a local bedsit taking up menial jobs - pot washing being one of them.

Beautiful, vivacious Rachel Nickell, out walking with her two-year-old son Alex on 15 July 1992, was attacked on Wimbledon Common and stabbed to death in a frenzied attack. She sustained forty-nine stab wounds; to be found later with her son clinging on to her lifeless body by retired architect, Michael Murry. This case was not fully solved until the use of DNA profiling discovered in 1953.

Napper used the Green Chain Link walk stretching from the Thames to Nunhead Cemetery, hence the moniker the 'Green Chain Link Killer'. Stalking women, hiding in plain sight secluded parts this area was Napper's preferred location being so close to his home. The Green Chain Link walk is broking up into eleven sections and includes numerous parks that provide museums, gardens, and the Thames barrier. It is easy to locate and well signposted with the distinctive 'G-C logo'.

1986 was noted as Nappers first crime having used an air gun to shoot at a local in the backside. He received a conditional discharge from the police. Now, Napper was on a rampage; some say up to seventy attacks on women over a ten-year period, others doubt it, but one thing is for sure Napper had an appetite for rape and murder. One thing stands out was the murder of Rachel Nickel Smith some have compared this murder to that of the East End Jack the Ripper in the frenzied way it was carried out. Could Jack the Ripper have had a bed in Broadmoor? It was noted that a patient by the name of James Kelly born 20 April 1860, was in Broadmoor for murdering his wife of seventeen days He was charged with aggravated homicide, being assessed Kelly was first thought to have been fit to stand trial being found guilty. He was sentenced to death, but the superintendent of Broadmoor was involved and had Kelly assessed and declared insane. Round about the time of the Ripper murders in Whitechapel East London, Kelly had escaped from Broadmoor by fabricating a key out of a metal pin. Some believe today he was Jack the Ripper, nonetheless Kelly remained at large until 1927 when he handed himself in at Broadmoor begging for a bed. Will we ever know the identity of Jack the Ripper may be not.

With a seemingly trustworthy gaze, Napper. slim build, black hair slightly balding, pouting lips gives one the impression of innocence. He had served an eight-week sentence for possession of a firearm in October 1992, having been ruled out as being responsible for the rapes and attacks along The Green Chain Walk - the Metropolitan Polices' attention were on six other suspects. Two of Nappers neighbours had suggested to the police that he suited the photo fit and description, but this was not taken up.

In 1993 Samantha Bisset was violently stabbed in the neck and chest area then sexually assaulted in her Plumstead home. It is thought that Napper had spent time stalking her and peering through the flat window on various occasions even when she was with her then boyfriend having sex. Napper then assaulted and smothered her four-year-old daughter in her bed. The sick twisted killer then mutilated Samantha's body like Jack the Ripper victims - cut from navel to the throat and posing her body in a suggestive pose. After the murder Napper took away body parts in a holdall as some sort of trophy. Her then boyfriend returned not believing what he had seen and initially thought it was staged. The body of the child officers described as looking like a young girl sleeping. This was one of the most despicable crimes the Metropolitan Police had come across and affected officers so deeply they took early retirement or two years absence off duty. It was not until 1995 that Napper was arrested after fingerprints was recovered from the flat of Samantha Bisset. Oddly, Napper had time to take detailed notes in a diary of what he was doing, including areas and descriptions of the attacks he was carrying out. At the time Colin Stagg was charged with Rachel's following a botched police sting operation involving a female officer, he pleaded his innocence and there was no evidence to suggest he did commit the crime. A honey trap set up by the Metropolitan police using a female under the name of Lizzie James was forced upon Stagg who thought she was interested in him. The reality was Lizzie was entrusted to gain Staggs's confidence and persuade him to reveal all so that the police could incriminate him in the murder of Racheal. Stagg was cleared and released after a year on remand in 1994, and received a substantial compensation pay out. Even though Napper on two occasions was asked to turn up to give blood he never did. Napper's DNA from Rachels body was matched in 2004 after the Metropolitan police ask LGC Forensics to conduct a review on her murder. In 2006 Napper was interviewed in Broadmoor but denied all involvement in her murder. In 2007, an independent review ruled out any contamination of any DNA samples and the police now had their man in their sights. Napper was charged with Rachel Nickell's murder. He pled guilty to manslaughter of Rachel in 2008 on the widely used diminished responsibility mitigation. Napper had a pair of size nine footwear which was seized by the police while being interviewed in Broadmoor. They were matched to the foot moulds taken by the river after Rachel's murder all bolstering the evidence against him. Napper is one of the cases that the psychiatric profession believes he is worthy of the Broadmoor treatment - there are those who think otherwise. A man who took meticulous notes on each victim, having two A to Z's with detailed spots of where he attacked his victims. For someone to take detailed notes shows some modicum of intelligence and awareness of what they were doing, so it cannot be said that he legally insane. Napper is a loner and refuses to respond to letters or communication with anyone outside of the hospital. His days are spent reading and given the chance gardening; gaunt, balding thin in appearance now, he still maintains his silence. Women staff have often said Napper comes across as friendly polite, the butter would not melt in his mouth type. Napper is one of those who will never leave Broadmoor only a few have ever served out their entire life in the hospital whether he will ever talk about the crimes or reveal what really happened stays with him – most certainly not. Racheal Nickell will never be forgotten and her son and his father re-visited the crime scene which was filmed by ITV and the memory of that day will never leave them. Now living their life abroad, let us praise Andre Alex's father who has raised a truly remarkable young man.

***

Summary.

'You don't change the course of history by turning the faces of portraits to the wall.'

Jawaharlal Nehru (1889-1964).

Broadmoor started its journey from an asylum in 1863 with the intention of being seen as a front runner for the *care* of the mostly the criminally mentally ill. Splendid for its era with fresh paint then and the fresh open air that breezed through the vast grounds. Roll on to 2019, and that care is still a constant as Christopher notes in the first lines of his Prologue, with even more fresh paint along with new concrete and paving; a bright coloured glass entrance hall with floors you could eat your dinner off. Surrounded by glistening impenetrable steel wire illuminated at night, now gone are the grim, high red brick walls, at night s one strolls around the perimeter, it is certainly the jewel in the crown for the treatment of many who are totally of unsound mind.

This is the new Broadmoor hospital, and us Brits should be proud because Broadmoor is without any doubt one of the finest of its type to be found anywhere across the world. But let us not shy from the history of the old for this is what makes the hospital stronger and better for all the learning it has achieved.

Was there any foresight how things would have progressed through the century and decades that followed? Would they ever see into the future or predict how people would react? We must remember the Victorian vision was far different than the vision we have today. But none-the-less it was a start as the Victorians had a very different perception on mental health and disabilities. In today's climate we treat mental health far differently then back then.

The actress Margaret Rutherford (1892-1972), born Balham, London, played' Miss Marple' in various films, her own father once a patient of Broadmoor. Broadmoor is a learning curve that just seems to curve and curve and is lifetime's work for many. You would think with all this danger within the hospital that staff would shy away with fear but so many have told me that it is the best job in the world. Security staff show bundles of pride working within walls, locked doors and long shifts secure and are on the ball. Never call it a prison the offence that staff take at any notion it is offends them all and rightly so. The old hospital gave the impression with the green window bars along with vast walls and barbed wire it was. Today's hospital is clean and crisp with technology to match monitoring patients 24/7 with Digital Care assistant by Oxhealth. This means the staff can monitor contact free and become alert to any problems arising. Sixteen new wards with clear line of sight and spacious to maximize the use of natural light. The wire and wall will never change double security fencing and modern lighting to cover areas that are vulnerable.

The staff never trust patients or turn their backs for a second and they watch out for each other. 3,700 staff work in Broadmoor from cleaners to cooks, nurses, security, and not let us forget the doctors. It is an ethos that builds a safe working environment. Nowadays, staff are located here for training before sending them on their way to various other establishments throughout the UK. Closed doors from the outside world not even a whisper from staff revealing anything except when it suits them.

The Victorians loved fresh air and rhubarb believing this was the way to cure many mental ills, followed by electric shock treatment and more fresh air in the vast gardens with views of the moor upon which it stands. Men and women mixed and daring not to upset the superintendent or staff for fear of being held in alone rooms or cells. The development of drugs and new forms of treatment practiced on those who were deemed to need it. Looking back from the first day of opening the asylum in 1863 to the present hospital which is light clean and colourful along with the absence of bars on the windows. Broadmoor's journey has been eventful, morphing into today's fit for purpose unit. But not everything went smoothly, nor does it today but it is not for the want of trying though. Yes, the department of health, who once used the 'let us throw them into Broadmoor because we cannot find anywhere else to place them,' has gone but one thing constant throughout Broadmoor's often chequered history – a dedicated, and humanitarian need to care for the mentally ill.

***

Acknowledgements.

My best friend and wife Chrissy. Ty & Tamsin Coster. The Monster in law Joan, Tony & Anne Coster, Sharon & Paul Calcutt, Jade Evie and Jack Leggett, Ryan & Charlotte Calcutt, Amy & Britney, Shelia Bartlett, Tom & Jenny & Josie, Paul Garrington, Dave Bradforth, Janet & David Bradforth, Emma Louise Fullford.

Mike Fear, Dave Cochrane, Mark Tovey, Colin Balfour,

Raychel Andrews, Jeff Wright, Dave George,

Penny William's, Liza Chatfield, Scott Ballantyne,

Scott Finch, June Coster, Millar (Tina), Lynne Lorraine

Jenny Ballantyne, Barry & jean Hodgkinson, Sheenagh & Gary,

Paul Richards, Angela Horsted, Paul Bessant,

Joe Jackie & the Girls, Adam Ord, Cliff Brigend,

Debbie Brigend, Brenden Smith, Kelly Smith, Fernsey (Mark),

John Morrow, Sadie Wilson Nonie, The Lovejoy's Matt Holly and Kids, Phil Tomlin,

Ade Lewis, Jason Lewis, Mike Read, Pip Salt, Nicole Badger,

Charlie Crayden, Carley Buddy & James Trezise, Charles & Sue Haskell,

Bruce Mason, Steve McCullough, Julie Mathews, Moo & John Page, Martin

Garlick, Clive Sturdy, Cristy Davis,

Dale Stockwell, Erica Wise, Gill Wilson, Helen Leather,

Jan Whitlock, Janet Walkley, Jason George, Pete Horseman,

Mark Merryweather, Nicky Lee, Nicki Clements, Perry Birtle,

Stuart Everett, Wayne Tippet. The Blairs.

And the world's No.1 true crime author Christopher Berry-Dee who pushed
me to the limit and I appreciate it big time.

Love you all Boris.

****